the 7 Essential Steps to Successful eBay® Marketing

Creative Strategies to Boost Profits Now

Janelle Elms
Phil Dunn
Amy Balsbaugh

McGraw-Hill

New York   Chicago   San Francisco
Lisbon   London   Madrid   Mexico City   Milan
New Delhi   San Juan   Seoul   Singapore
Sydney   Toronto

The **McGraw-Hill** Companies

McGraw-Hill books are available at special quantity discounts to use as premiums and sales promotions, or for use in corporate training programs. For more information, please write to the Director of Special Sales, Professional Publishing, McGraw-Hill, Two Penn Plaza, New York, NY 10121-2298. Or contact your local bookstore.

The 7 Essential Steps to Successful eBay® Marketing: Creative Strategies to Boost Profits Now

1234567890 DOC DOC 0198765

ISBN 0-07-226091-2

Vice President & Group Publisher	Philip Ruppel
Vice President & Publisher	Jeffrey Krames
Acquisitions Editor	Marjorie McAneny
Project Editor	LeeAnn Pickrell
Acquisitions Coordinator	Agatha Kim
Copy Editor	Lisa Theobald
Proofreader	Susie Elkind
Indexer	Karin Arrigoni
Composition	ITC
Illustrator	ITC
Creative Director	Scott Jackson
Cover Design	Jeff Weeks

This book was composed with Adobe® InDesign®.

About the Authors

Janelle Elms is a lead instructor touring nationwide with eBay University. A Silver PowerSeller on eBay (http://www.JanelleElms.com), she has recently wrapped up production on a new training video for eBay called *Beyond the Basics*. Janelle's work with eBay has extended to teaching pilot training programs, including a leading-edge program initiated by Senator Hillary Rodham Clinton that is designed to help small towns understand how to sell globally instead of just locally.

Creator of the exclusive eBay 101 and 102 classes taught throughout the United States, Janelle has helped numerous individuals build successful businesses on eBay. To date, she has trained more than 20,000 people in eBay sales, marketing, customer service, and customer-retention strategies. Janelle specializes in corporate consulting designed to teach companies how to develop or maximize an eBay sales channel.

Co-author of the best-selling *eBay Your Business: Maximize Sales and Get Results* (McGraw-Hill, 2004), Janelle also self-published two eBay how-to books, *Don't Throw It Away Sell It On eBay!,* and *No Seriously, What Do You Really Do For a Living?* She has also started several eBay community groups in the Pacific Northwest, including the eBay for Beginners and eBay PowerSellers groups in her hometown of Seattle. As a national and corporate speaker and educator, Janelle believes that the eBay opportunity is available for all who seek to become a part of this global community.

Phil Dunn is a marketing and advertising writer/consultant. Since the early 1990s Phil has been producing marketing collateral, white papers, success stories, trade show production scripts, flash presentations, magazine ads, and radio advertising for Fortune 500 companies (including Microsoft, Hewlett-Packard, Pitney Bowes, IKON, and Toshiba Medical), as well as for small- and medium-sized businesses. Using persuasive writing and time-honored marketing approaches, he has sold everything from $22 haircuts to $50,000 cars to $1 million software licensing agreements. His company, Synapse Services Co., specializes in "turning complex subjects into everyday benefits."

Synapse hosts several blogs (and RSS feeds) that deal with persuasive writing techniques, sales fundamentals, marketing strategy, and eBay marketing. A free newsletter that covers similar topics is available at the company site as well (http://www.qualitywriter.com). Synapse offers consulting and copywriting services to companies that need to enhance their eBay presence and pull more profits out of the channel.

Phil has a Master of Arts in print journalism (with public relations and broadcast media training) from the University of Southern California and a Bachelor of Arts in History from UC Berkeley. He's a surfer, an ice hockey player, an obsessive-compulsive reader, a confounded fiction writer, a proud and giddy father, and a "good listener" who followed his wife's advice when she said, "Go follow your dreams, write a book, get published!"

The daughter of an antiques dealer, **Amy Balsbaugh** (http://www.redfishantiques.com) has been involved in the antiques and collectibles business since childhood. With the rise of eBay's popularity in the late 1990s, Amy closed her brick-and-mortar antiques shop in San Francisco and began selling on eBay exclusively.

The benefits of selling on eBay were immediately apparent. Auction-format listings frequently sparked bidding wars that escalated final gavel prices far beyond the price tags in her former shop. Overhead expenses for online selling were significantly less than the cost of pricey commercial real estate in San Francisco. And within a few months of selling on eBay, she had shipped goods to customers on six of seven continents (she's still waiting to find a customer in Antarctica!). She's continually delighted to meet cyber-customers who would have never graced the doorstep of her quaint brick-and-mortar shop. Plus, eBay's incredible database technology has allowed her to sell everything from a miniature Victorian die-cut valentine card to the entire estate of a renowned historian and collector of art and antiques.

As eBay has grown, so has Amy's business by taking advantage of new programs and features in the ever-expanding eBay landscape. A member of the PowerSeller program from its inception, Amy is proud of her more than 5,000 feedback comments with 100% positive ratings. Like the multitudes of others who have made eBay selling a full-time profession, Amy uses the power of eBay to achieve success in her business, while enjoying the freedom of self-employment.

Contents

To all the incredible, creative, unstoppable eBay entrepreneurs
who make business fun and keep eBay
a vibrant place to sell.

Acknowledgments

Many minds and talents make up a book, and they don't all make it onto the cover, of course. We'd like to thank Margie McAneny, our editor, for shepherding this project from its infancy to its ballyhooed coming out party at eBay Live and beyond. She led with class and patience at the most challenging junctures, and contributed keen observations and guidance when we needed it most. She championed our cause valiantly throughout the complex ranks of McGraw-Hill. Roger Stewart from McGraw-Hill deserves our heartfelt gratitude for acting as the project's initial catalyst by contacting Margie and promoting our concept. Special thanks goes to Sally Richards, the most connected networker, writer, and technology guru we know, for introducing us to Roger.

LeeAnn Pickrell, our senior project editor, deserves mighty applause and thanks for seeing the book with an engineer's logic and an artist's sense of pace and flow. She connected concepts that we overlooked and asked the tough questions that only fresh readers ponder (and authors overlook). Thank you Jody McKenzie for assuming the role of LeeAnn when she was out of town—you were phenomenal. Agatha Kim, our acquisitions coordinator, pulled the whole project together with grace, speed, and tact. Thanks for your editing contributions, as well. Lisa Theobald, our copy editor, got into the trenches and our minds, fixing our goofs, clarifying obscured concepts, and generally honing the book so that it reads like butter. Many thanks to you.

Much gratitude goes to Kate Viotto, senior marketing manager, and Bettina Faltermeier, publicity manager. As fellow marketers, we know that your efforts make the world spin and the books fly off the shelves. Without your hard work, we'd be lost in the stacks.

We'd also like to thank those practitioners and researchers of human behavior, psychology, and marketing science who came before us. These include several icons of the industry, including David Ogilvy, John Caples, Dr. Robert Cialdini, and Robert Bly. Without these great minds, advertising and marketing would be stuck in some stone-age morass.

Finally, each of our family members deserves the warmest thanks for their support throughout a long year of late nights and extended writing jags.

Introduction

I believe eBay in the next 25 years secedes from the union, becomes its own independent city-state, and is a better managed and stronger political entity than the U.S. federal government.

—The Motley Fool Stock Advisor

---

eBay has changed dramatically in the past decade. What began as a small online marketplace for collectibles has grown to cover a wide array of mid to upscale markets and person-to-person sales that span the globe. In the old days, an eBay seller could write up a quick description of an item, take a few digital photos, upload the information to eBay, and wait for bids to come in. Those of us who were selling on eBay in the early days found that it was easy money.

But in recent years, the competition has become fierce. Tens of thousands of new sellers have entered the eBay marketplace, including large-scale retailers with the edge of professional marketing expertise and power-house corporate experience. The eBay market has also been flooded with small-time sellers, who sell at low margins for little profit and make it difficult for other sellers to compete with their prices.

eBay has also made system changes offering new selling formats, advanced tools, and eBay Stores. While the system changes have provided new opportunities for selling—many sellers have found it necessary to adapt quickly or quickly perish.

To succeed, you need to hone your skills in a wide range of disciplines. You need to discover what will make a buyer bid on your item, rather than an identical one being sold by a competitor. You need to understand what motivates a buyer, and what prompts people to click on the "Bid" or "Buy-It-Now" button. You need to know what makes a listing visually appealing and how to inspire confidence in your professionalism.

The 7 Essential Steps to Successful eBay Marketing takes proven strategies used by marketing and business management professionals and retools them for eBay-specific selling. Previously, this information was privy only to eBay sellers who had a background in advertising, or who had the patience to trudge through dry marketing textbooks. This fast-paced, conversational book presents these valuable insights in a format that's memorable and fun to read. You'll discover a wealth of new information in less time than it takes to read a pulp novel.

When you finish you'll be able to:

- Understand buyers and position your products for faster, higher margin sales
- Present products more persuasively (in visual and in written form)
- Inform prospects while nudging them toward PayPal
- Grab attention, make offers, and close the sale
- Understand keyword searches so you can draw in more traffic
- Create urgency and sweeten the deal
- Unlock the collector mindset to maximize sales on uncommon or coveted items
- Organize your eBay Store so it's easy to navigate and visually appealing
- Differentiate your business from competitors
- Cultivate loyal customers and build positive feedback
- Customize and automate customer communications to build loyalty and repeat business
- And so much more

There are a number of decent eBay instructional books on the market today, but they limit their scope to the mechanics of selling on eBay and navigating the Web site. They're chock full of screenshot illustrations and "click here to do this" sort of information. However, the subject of marketing is discussed sparsely, and they offer few new insights.

We're here to show you how to persuasively and professionally present your products while building a solid, memorable, "sticky" brand within eBay. We give you step-by-step instructions in niche marketing, brand-building, customer service and retention, planning strategies for growth, and more. We fill the void left by other eBay instructional books, offering insight into the finer points of marketing products and forging a strong eBay business.

WHO SHOULD READ THIS BOOK?

The 7 Essential Steps to Successful eBay Marketing was created for any eBay seller who would like to see their business grow, work more efficiently, and find healthier bottom lines. It's for any eBay seller interested in honing their marketing skills and improving sales in their established businesses. Whether you're a PowerSeller, an antiques trader, a corporate product manager looking for a new sales channel, or a reformed pack rat cleaning out your garage, this book helps you enhance the quality of your eBay listings while boosting sales volume and profit margins.

For the newcomer to eBay, the book makes an excellent companion to one of the eBay primer books that exist on the market. More seasoned eBay sellers who need to revamp and improve their business to compete in the evolving eBay marketplace may stand to gain the most by reading this book. It's written for those who may have already made a few mistakes and want to find a better, smarter way of doing business. It's also for those who have already achieved a degree of success and would like to see that success reinforced with some advertising science.

The book's no-nonsense style boils down complex marketing philosophies and practices into casual and easy-to-read text that applies specifically to selling on eBay. It's written to be accessible to those without a background in business or marketing. However, even MBAs will find the strategies engaging and the approaches refreshing. Anyone actively selling on eBay will find rock-solid advice and immediately applicable wisdom by simply flipping through the chapters.

HOW THIS BOOK IS ORGANIZED

The path to eBay success is divided into 7 essential steps. Each chapter of this book is devoted to a different strategy.

Chapter 1: Make a Plan: Your First Step to Success

We begin the book the way any business executive launches a marketing effort—by performing a market analysis and creating a marketing plan. This chapter gives you an easy to follow plan for your own market analysis. We cover subjects such as:

- Discovering a niche market
- Identifying your target demographic
- Understanding your products and how to position them effectively
- Assessing your competition
- Forging your own unique eBay brand

Chapter 2: Seller's Toolbox: Use eBay and Other Resources to Increase Sales

We mentioned previously that this book focuses on selling strategy rather than being a traditional "how-to" instruction book. With that said, however, we found it essential to provide a chapter that focused on some of the advanced tools that are offered by eBay and other third-party services. These tools help you work more efficiently and market your goods more effectively. They help you showcase your professionalism while assisting you in amassing your fortune. Disclosed in this chapter are secret tips, pointers, and notes about special services and new features, including:

- Listing creation and management tools
- Cool tools to help manage sales
- eBay Stores
- Tools to help with marketing and promotions
- Customer service tools

With the staggering array of tools available to eBay sellers, we also offer advice on ways to separate the wheat from the chaff and pick the tools that will work best for your individual business.

Chapter 3: Putting a Face on Your eBay Brand: Critical Presentation and Visual Techniques

Today's Web users are savvier than ever, and they demand aesthetically pleasing and intuitively designed Web sites. eBay listings are no exception to this rule. This chapter shows you how to build a brand, develop a consistent graphic identity, organize pages, and develop a visual connection with your prospects and customers. We uncover secrets of professional Web and graphic designers and mesh those insights with commonsense content advice. Included are discussions on:

- Building a graphic identity for your business
- Creating an effective logo
- Designing your eBay listings and eBay Store
- Using your brand in printed materials and packaging

This chapter also shows you how to pull all these elements together to create a cohesive selling identity that customers find deeply compelling.

Chapter 4: Sell Anyone Anything with Words: Effective Copywriting Techniques

Many eBay sellers admit that writing item descriptions is one of the more tedious tasks of running an eBay business. However, when competition is tight, a strong item description can mean the difference between making the sale and losing out to a competitor. Fortunately, if you know some of the secrets of professional advertising copywriters, writing can be fast, easy, and relatively painless. Uncovered in this chapter are some tricks of the trade that help maximize the sales potential of your item descriptions, including:

- Understanding customer needs
- Describing product features and benefits

- Using a conversational tone
- Creating FAQs
- Crafting effective keyword titles
- Fine-tuning your item descriptions

Chapter 5: Advanced Marketing Strategies: Extra-Mile Salesmanship for High-Ticket Sales

Big-league selling requires a sales style that incorporates persuasion, expertise, and experience. In this chapter, we show you how to infuse your listings with all three of these—turning your pages into comfortable, informative, and enticing propositions to visitors. You'll see how techniques used by experienced salespeople in the traditional retail world can be used just as effectively in the flat, text-and-photo world of eBay. We'll discuss ways to:

- Tap into the power of scarcity to drive sales
- Use your authority and expertise to sell goods
- Include testimonials that move products
- Integrate storytelling and problem solving in item descriptions
- Make offers, close the deal, and up-sell or cross-sell for bigger profits

This chapter also shows you how to promote your items within eBay and use search engine optimization techniques to boost traffic from the Internet at large.

Chapter 6: Customer Satisfaction and Retention: The Holy Grail of eBay Sales

Good customer service is the cornerstone to a successful eBay business. Not only does it ensure the satisfaction of the customer the first time they shop with you, it also encourages them to return to shop with you again. Customer retention is the art of luring your customers back to buy more, and mastering it is a direct path to success. This chapter examines the building blocks of good customer service, as well as strategies the pros use to keep customers coming back. Included are discussions on:

- Earning the customer's trust
- Communicating effectively and shipping promptly
- Personalizing customer relationships
- Leaving and receiving feedback
- Creating newsletters and e-mail campaigns
- Offering gifts that inspire reciprocation
- Developing promotions and incentives for return business

Chapter 7: Take It to the Next Level: Charting Your Course,
Measuring Success, Planning for the Future

The final chapter helps you take the lessons from the other six chapters to craft a plan of action that will lead you down the path of success. This chapter contains advice that will help you:

- Set goals and timelines for implementing marketing strategies
- Measure the effectiveness of your marketing actions
- Identify and improve on the strategies that work for you
- Plan for business growth
- Continue to learn, evolve, and prosper

Finally, this book is peppered with plenty of tips, notes, and cautions that tap into the wealth of knowledge of marketing experts and eBay insiders. We've also included plenty of quotes—some that highlight key areas of the text and others that share sage advice from noted marketing gurus. With just a few tips, you'll improve your eBay selling dramatically. A world of fun and profit awaits you . . . so let's get started!

Chapter 1

Make a Plan: Your First Step to Success

As you read this book, eBay is moving merchandise at a rate of more than $62,000 a minute (and growing). Every day 111,000 e-commerce–savvy sellers join eBay to sell their wares. This is a worldwide free-market phenomenon. eBay is the most successful Web site and the most popular shopping destination in the world; 4.4 million transactions occur on eBay every day, and the aggregate eBay economy traded $34 billion worth of goods in 2004. There's a lot going on at this humble "little" commerce hub.

As a seller, you need every competitive edge you can muster, so we begin the book by discussing how you can plan for success. Whether you're just starting out or you've been selling on eBay for years, whether you're a one-person shop or a company with hundreds of employees, this chapter will help you map out and refocus your overall business plan and approach to the market. Let's dive right in.

In the corporate world, executives create marketing plans as a means of forging their paths to success. These plans often use fancy marketing-speak, with terms like *market analysis* and *competitive analysis, branding* and *identity*. If you have a background in business, these terms are probably familiar. However, if you don't have an MBA, there's no need to be intimidated. Performing your own market analysis of eBay is not so difficult. But even if you already have a strong foothold in the business world, this chapter shows you several new and refreshing marketing approaches.

Planning your own success just boils down to the thoughtful analysis of a few basic considerations:

- Know who you are.
- Know your products.
- Know your customers.
- Know your competition.
- Know how to tie it all together.

1

Know Who You Are

eBay's trademarked slogan is "The World's Online Marketplace." eBay is an economy unto itself. But eBay also describes its millions of users with the intimate term *community*. If you think about it, the idea of a community is really not that far off the mark.

Compare the eBay community and opportunities to the community of your own town or city and the opportunities for buying and selling where you live. Step out your front door and you may find your neighbor having a garage sale. Walk down to your mom-and-pop corner store for some daily necessity, or frequent a medium-sized specialty shop for a hard-to-find item. Hop on the freeway and drive to the mall or a big-box superstore for a broad selection or a bargain.

Just as in your real-world community, eBay sellers represent the wide spectrum of the resale, retail, and wholesale world. On eBay, you will find a range of sellers—from those cleaning out their attics to sell items for extra cash to Fortune 500 companies expanding their sales to capitalize on the eBay phenomenon, and just about everything in between. Now's the time to examine where exactly you fit into this virtual community.

Motivations

Not to get too cosmic or metaphysical here, but understanding where you're coming from is the first step in understanding where you're going. Your motivations for becoming a part of the eBay community are a big part of defining yourself and your business.

Some folks sell on eBay as an alternative revenue stream. eBay is a great moonlighting job for many people, and others, such as stay-at-home parents and retirees, use eBay to supplement their incomes. Some people come to eBay with the dream of self-employment. They've discovered the joy of the "10-second commute" from the kitchen to the computer, and they relish the freedom of setting their own hours and being their own boss.

Owners of traditional brick-and-mortar retail businesses often join eBay to create an online selling presence without having to go through the rigors and expense of developing and marketing their own Web sites. The online community helps them expand their customer base from a limited regional area to the entire world. This broader base of customers on eBay sometimes leads brick-and-mortar businesses to abandon the storefront completely and sell only through a virtual store. Other sellers have existing e-commerce businesses and come to eBay to increase sales and locate new customers.

There are as many reasons for starting (or continuing) an eBay business as there are eBay sellers. Whatever your reasons, answering the "What brings you to eBay?" question is the first step in creating a solid marketing plan.

Finding a Niche Market

Many sellers find that eBay gives them the opportunity to turn their hobbies or passions into money-making endeavors. Other sellers with businesses existing outside of eBay have already found their paths to success by carving out their own specialties or areas of expertise. These two scenarios are closely related, because they both capitalize on niche markets. The term *niche market* is a buzzword that gets tossed around frequently, and it really just means pitching a specific product or service to a narrowly defined group of customers.

Niche marketing is positioning a specific product or service to a specialized and focused portion of the market.

Most businesses start by catering to a niche market. Countless entrepreneurs found their beginnings in fields of their own personal interest, where they identified a product or service that like-minded people needed or desired. Look at all the new-fangled baby care products on the market, from frontloading baby packs to goofy mobiles that mount to car seats. Many of these products were invented by parents for their own babies. They know from their own experience that other parents would appreciate the products, too.

Discovering Your Niche

A great thing about eBay is that it can be easy to find your niche market and cater to this group of people (or your niche market might find you). Take a close look at the broad list of eBay categories and subcategories. Figure 1-1 captures just a small portion of this very long list. Each category is a niche market unto itself, and eBay is the broad marketplace that holds together these subdivided markets. All these special-interest niche groups are like little side streets on the eBay highway.

You can buy everything from computer equipment, to cars, houses, and services on eBay. For the sake of analogy, think of eBay as a humongous bazaar with thousands of booths with individual vendors, each selling a very specific item—everything from copper cooking pots, to fabric, exotic spices, fruits and vegetables, to hand-crafted and other interesting goods. The market is teeming with customers, each seeking something different. No single seller can possibly meet all the needs of all those customers, so each of these smart vendors specializes in a specific product that he or she knows intimately.

This connection among the proprietor, a product, and its customers has allowed a centuries-old retailing system to survive—and thrive—in the modern age. Smart eBay sellers will find a niche market and then work to be the very best in the minds of a small group of avid customers. By being specialized, these sellers can keep their fingers on the pulse of their niche market,

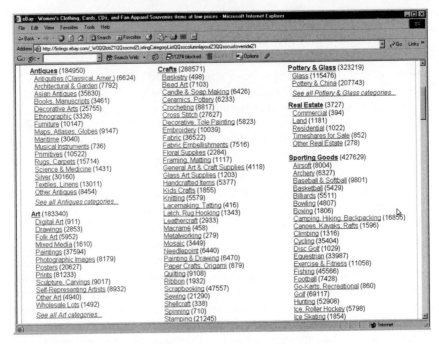

Figure 1-1 This partial list of categories demonstrates the broad variety of niche markets that exists on eBay.

maintaining an intimate connection with the desires and demands of their customers.

Think about your own interests or areas of expertise and how they are reflected in the products you sell on eBay. Perhaps you're a technophile who sells computer parts, or a movie buff who sells DVDs and videos. Maybe you're an avid traveler who returns home with treasures from around the world to sell on eBay. Many sellers in the antiques and collectibles fields are also collectors themselves and use eBay as a means of thinning their possessions and earning extra money to make new purchases.

These examples illustrate individuals selling on eBay; however, businesses of all sizes also need to develop well-defined areas of expertise and create their own niches. If your business employs 2 people, 10 people, or 200, the scope of your business is still guided by your own interests and passions as the "chief of the tribe." The important thing is that you convey your expertise to your team members. They, too, must understand your specific niche market to be able to address the needs and desires of your customers in the best ways.

Niche Is Not Always Defined by Products

Maybe you don't think you have a specialty or you don't fit in any easily categorized niche. Think a little harder. The *way* you do business can be your niche. You might ship faster than anyone else. Maybe you're known as someone who can find any product at lower than retail price. Perhaps you're a champ at refurbishing old things and making them look new again. Maybe you have a connection who can get hold of sold-out tickets for sporting events or concerts.

An entire group of sellers on eBay, known as *trend wavers,* closely follow trends and jump from one niche market to another. When a particular item is hot, they'll sell the heck out of it, and then they'll jump out of that market and onto the next big wave. They always have the hottest toy for the holidays or the coolest fashion of the season. These sellers have a knack for being one step ahead of what buyers want, and they have found their niche in forecasting fads and fashions for profit.

Specialty doesn't have to be tied to a finite product set or a narrowly defined product line. The important thing is that you define what makes your business unique and communicate it to your potential customers as well as your employees.

Tip: Take the time now with a pen and paper and define your niche market in writing. An intimate knowledge of your niche will be helpful as you progress through this book. All of the discussions on copywriting and advanced marketing techniques should be understood within the context of your niche.

Maintaining Niche Focus

Equally as important as finding a niche is continuing to grow and profit within that specific market. Many businesses have faltered or failed in attempts to diversify beyond a tight niche market. The sirens of opportunity can be tempting, but it's important to remember that drifting from your niche can be deadly as your business grows. If you are known for selling great hamburgers, don't get into tofu. If you sell teen fashions, don't entertain delusions of complete clothing market domination and stray into the 65-plus demographic.

The sirens of opportunity can be tempting, but it's important to remember that drifting from your niche can be deadly as your business grows.

Develop the Principles and Goals of Your Business

Corporate players large and small frequently develop *vision statements* or *mission statements,* fancy terms for defining the scope and philosophy of a business. At first consideration, these kinds of exercises might sound like colossal time-wasters, especially for a small business that's consumed with the countless daily tasks of running a business. However, self-examination works wonders for a business, whether you're a one-person shop or you employ a small army. Defined principles and goals set the tone for internal standards and expectations, and they also do wonders for projecting your organization out into the market. "Know thyself" is one of the most overly quoted instructions on the planet for a reason.

Don't worry though, because writing your own mission statement doesn't need to be a painful experience. The secret is to keep your mission statement simple. You want to capture your essence, reality, and ambitions without popping a blood vessel in the process. All it takes is a little brainstorming. Everybody loves brainstorming. It's work, but it sure doesn't feel like it.

Sit down with a pen and paper, and write down your ideas as they come to mind. For starters, ask yourself the following questions about your business:

- Aside from making you money, what is the broader purpose of your business?
- What do you want to achieve with your eBay business?
- What is your benefit to selling on eBay versus other retail venues?
- What do you sell? What's special or unique about your products?
- What do you want for your employees? Do they want the same things you do? Be sure to incorporate their perceptions into your consideration.
- How can you tie these musings back to your customers? How does what you want intersect with what your market niche desires?
- Think backward, from the customer to the innards of your organization. What's the value of your product, and why do people come to you for it?

Some businesses develop mission statements that are several paragraphs long, with elaborate lists of their core beliefs, goals, the ways they value their customers, and on and on. If you end up getting that detailed, that's great; however, it's not really necessary. Your mission statement doesn't need to be so significant that it realigns the planets. Just make it meaningful and inspiring to you and your employees, and be sure that it will make sense to your customers, too.

Here are a few sample mission statements that might help to get those creative juices flowing:

- **Sporting goods**　"Turning couch potatoes into athletes."
- **Antiques**　"Connecting collectors with the objects of their desire."
- **Costume jewelry**　"Exquisite adornments at affordable prices."

- **Prints and posters** "Creating the museum experience at home with high-quality fine art reproductions."
- **Trendy clothing** "The latest fashions from the runway, delivered to your doorway."
- **Music** "Our staff of music experts uncover rare recordings, coveted imports, and early releases to please the discerning ears of our customers."

If you're up against that miserable, unyielding blank page, or the humbling writer's block that turns writers into cappuccino aficionados and cigarette hobbyists, then think about some of the brands you already know. A lot of the popular companies boil down their principles and goals to short, snappy phrases. For years, Nike's corporate mantra has been "Authentic athletic performance." Starbucks uses "Rewarding everyday moments." These are great examples, because they capture both internal expectations and customer benefits. They're ingenious, too, because Nike isn't just about shoes and Starbucks isn't just about coffee. These statements don't pigeonhole the companies—they're wide open, yet focused.

Discovery Equals Growth

Sometimes discovery takes intention. When you intend to discover something important about your business, something that could possibly make you more money and make a stronger connection to your prospects and buyers, you inevitably succeed. Guaranteed—if you spend a half hour to an hour in a quiet place somewhere, you'll find out some things about yourself and your business that should be taped to your computer monitor or framed in a hallway plaque.

What you discover will be useful in a very practical, tangible sense, too. As we progress through this book, you'll have plenty of opportunities to apply your mission statement to your eBay business. You'll use it in your eBay Store, your e-mail signature, and other marketing efforts. And the discoveries you make will be applied to every communication you have with customers, from the items you put up on the auction block to the follow-up e-mails you send to satisfied customers.

Tip: Don't gloss over your mission statement. You'll need it later in the book as we get into more detail with your eBay marketing efforts.

What's in a Name?

"That which we call a rose by any other name would smell as sweet." Well, maybe that worked for Shakespeare, but in the business world, your name is pretty darn important. It serves as both a first impression and the foundation for branding efforts and market perception. Your business name is a marketing tool that needs to convey in a few short words the message of who you are and what you sell. It needs to convey your business's mission or vision.

If your business is fairly new, you've probably recently experienced the exquisite angst that choosing a name can generate. Or perhaps you've been using the same business name for years and have experienced varying degrees of satisfaction with the choice you've made. Whatever your situation, take some time and put forth the effort to assess how well your business name is working for you.

Take a few minutes to scrutinize your business name and ask yourself the following questions:

- *Is your business name easy to understand and remember?* It needs to be simple to pronounce and pleasant to hear. If you have an uncommon family name, the kind that telemarketers usually butcher, it's probably best to avoid using it as part of your business name.
- *Is your product line easily identified by your name?* Customers don't want to have to guess about what you're selling, so avoid being vague. "Poseidon's Pool Supplies" is a perfect example, because it has a catchy, mythological element, but it's also very clear about the line of products being sold. Including an indication of your product line in your business name also helps with search engine optimization—a strategy we will discuss in Chapter 2.
- *Does the* style *of your name reflect your business?* For example, a cutesy name like "Kitty Corner" would be great for someone selling pet supplies, but a business that sells high-end consumer electronics will need a name that is more cutting-edge, like "StereoTech" or "SoundLab."
- *Is your name too trendy?* You're going to need to grow with your business name, and you won't want it to sound dated in a few years. Consider the naming problem that 20th Century Fox encountered at the beginning of the new millennium.
- *Does your name pose any trademark infringement dilemmas?* Think of the legal wrath you may incur from the lawyers at a certain toy store chain if you name your business "Computers R Us." You can check the trademark status of business names by going to http://www.uspto.gov.
- *How unique is your name?* Searching for businesses with similar or identical fictitious business names is usually a part of the process of registering a business with local governmental authorities. However, it's equally important to check the uniqueness of your name in the eBay world.

You want to be sure that your business won't be confused with a different eBay business with a similar name. Here's an easy way to check this:

1. Go into the eBay search menu.
2. Select the Find Stores option from the options menu at the left.
3. Type in the name of your business in the text field.
4. Select the Store Name And Description option under the text field.
5. Click the Search button.

This will bring up a list of eBay Store names that are similar to yours. Hopefully, you won't be too surprised by what you find. But if you discover a business operating under a similar name with a poor feedback rating or a bizarre line of products, you might consider renaming your business.

You can also search by User ID:

1. Select the Advanced Search menu on the top-right corner of eBay's home page.
2. Click Search By Seller.
3. Type in the ID you are investigating.
4. If there's a matching ID, eBay will provide you with that person's auction/listing/store information, as well as a list of IDs similar to the one you are searching for.

Choosing a New Name

What if you find that your existing business name just isn't cutting the mustard? Don't panic. Choosing a new business name can be challenging, but a few simple steps will make the process easier:

1. Brainstorm all the keywords or descriptive terms that describe your business, your products, and your customers' desires. Be sure to include nouns, verbs, and adjectives. Don't be afraid to go a little crazy with your list. The more exhaustive your list, the more naming options you'll find.
2. See if any glaringly obvious names pop out at you. If not, use a thesaurus to look up words on your keyword list and make a second list of buzzwords that apply to your business. Did the thesaurus yield any name enlightenment?

3. Consider rhymes or alliterations (repeated first syllables)—like "Books for Cooks" for culinary literature, or "Origami Originals" for Japanese handmade papers.

4. Identify any parts of your own name that fit in with any of your buzzwords. How about "Bobblehead Bob" for sports memorabilia or "Shutterbug Sam" for camera equipment?

5. Use this process to think up a short list of name possibilities and try them out on your friends.

6. Review the questions posed earlier in this section. Is your new name a better fit for your business?

If your personal brainstorming efforts don't yield the perfect name, there's another way to do this, which is a bit more Web-hip. A number of different name generator sites let you plug in the keywords associated with your business, and the generators spit out dozens upon dozens of possible names. Two sites that are free of charge and offer basic naming suggestions are http://www.nameboy.com/ and http://www.dnwhiz.com/.

For more sophisticated business name and product name generation, the services don't come quite as cheap. NameBuilder (http://www.namexpress.com/namesoftware.html) and Name Razor (http://www.creative-name-generator.com) are popular programs. You'll need to pay a price ($35 to $100) to download these software programs, but if you're truly stuck, they can be the cure to your business-naming blues.

Your Business Name and eBay

Think about your business name as it relates to your eBay user ID and your e-mail address. Do these names accurately reflect your business? Do these elements work together fairly seamlessly? One of the main themes that will recur throughout this book is the importance of projecting consistency in your business. However, many sellers out there are still using old user IDs, like "bidding_maniac" or odd combinations of initials and zip codes that have little or no correlation to the name of their business. Even your e-mail address should work to convey your vision accurately.

If you're still using your old college e-mail address, PartyAnimal@ hotmail.com, think about what that says about your business and your professionalism. (Unless you're in the business of selling party supplies, in which case, the name is perfect!) It may not seem like such a big deal, but you want all aspects of your business name, including your user ID and your e-mail address, to be memorable to your customers.

If you need to change your eBay User ID, rest assured that all of your current feedback travels with you to your new ID. Changing your User ID is an easy process:

1. Log into your My eBay account.
2. Scroll down to Accounts on the left side and click on Personal Information.
3. Click on the Change button next to your current User ID.

Know Your Product

Now that you have a good grasp of *who* you are, let's take some time to get a deeper understanding of your products or services. What are you selling? What are its purpose, features, and selling points?

Ask a few more questions: Is your product a common necessity or a high-end luxury item? Bed linens, for example, are a very practical item—unless, of course, you're selling 1020 thread count imported Egyptian cotton sheets at $1000 a set. Describe its appearance: Is it an object of beauty or purely functional? Is it an oil painting or a potato peeler? Consider technological factors: Is it up-to-date? This can be incredibly important in selling computer items and other high-tech devices. And think about social factors: Is it trendy or a fad to be sold quickly before the fashion fades away, or is its appeal timeless? Think of the emotions your product evokes. The entire (and very successful) greeting card industry is based on emotions.

Finally, consider any issues of seasonality. We all know that the peak of demand for Christmas decorations falls in mid- to late November. However, seasonal nuances can exist with many different products. For example, if you sell superhero action figures, you may want to time your sales to coincide with the release of big summer movie blockbusters.

Also consider products in the marketplace that are similar to yours. Research other products that customers might buy instead of yours, and determine why your product is better. What benefits do your products offer that surpass those of similar items? Is it higher quality? Is it a new and improved version of an older product? Can you ship it faster than your competitors? Can you sell it at a cheaper price?

Pricing and Profit

Developing a pricing strategy is an important element in any market analysis or marketing plan. Pricing strategy can be extremely complex—full-semester courses are devoted to pricing as part of MBA studies, and countless volumes of business books deal with the subject. There are complicated theories and scientific formulas for pricing products, and people have created high-demand careers as pricing strategists.

But the good news is that there's really no reason to be intimidated by the prospect of pricing your goods for eBay. Since eBay prices are driven strongly by customers, many of these theories and formulas get thrown right out the window anyway. All you really need to price your products effectively for eBay is a basic understanding of a few factors and principles, and the time and patience to research and test.

Assessing Your Costs

The first step in determining prices for your products is a thoughtful analysis of all the costs involved in their sale. This includes not only your cost for acquiring or manufacturing the goods for sale, but also indirect costs such as overhead expenses (rent, utilities, ISP fees, eBay fees, and so on). You should also consider the costs of your fixed assets, such as your computers, digital camera, and other devices. Of course, if you have employees, you must assess the cost of their wages, payroll taxes, workers' compensation, insurance, and so on. Even if you have no employees and you're a lone wolf working from home, you still need to factor in the cost of your own labor. And think of those long lists of business expense deductibles that you itemize on your taxes. All those items need to be factored into your cost analysis.

Tip: Consider the cost of your own labor: Let's face it, you're not running a charity here. You need to be sure that you are going to earn money for your own time and effort.

Some sellers use their costs as the exclusive factor that drives their pricing decisions. This strategy is called *cost-plus pricing*. It takes the cost of goods sold and adds a percentage or flat-rate markup for profit to determine the final price. Despite the fact that many sellers use this pricing strategy, some inherent flaws exist in the cost-plus scheme. First, it assumes that you are going to sell all of the units on which you've based your price. If you end up selling less than expected, your profits will diminish exponentially.

Second, cost-plus pricing also doesn't account for the possibility that customers may be willing to pay more for your product than the price you've set. For example, if you determine a fixed price of $10 for your item, but eBay customers would actually be willing to pay $20, you're missing the opportunity to make an additional $10 per unit. This is where it becomes important to have a full understanding of the price that the eBay market will bear for your goods and incorporate it into your pricing strategy.

Understanding Demand

One of the amazing things about eBay is that it's nearly a pure market economy. With competition between bidders setting the prices on auction-style listings, and with the buyer's ease of comparison shopping for fixed priced items, the concepts of supply and demand are alive and well on eBay. This can make pricing on eBay a tricky endeavor. What sells for one price on a Tuesday night might sell for significantly more the following Sunday afternoon. It's a function of the number of interested buyers and the number of identical or similar items available at any given time. If the eBay market is flooded with tons of a particular item, it likely won't command premium prices. If the item is fairly rare, the bidding will often drive the price higher.

Note: We'll discuss scarcity and how to leverage it in Chapter 5.

Customer desires play a major role in setting prices by demand. Hotter-than-hot consumer goods are often in short supply in traditional markets, and sellers who carry these coveted items on eBay will command higher than retail prices. Apple iPods are a great example of this phenomenon. The iPod minis, in particular, command higher than retail prices on eBay (last we checked—but by the time this book goes to print, a new product will likely be kicking off bidding frenzies).

Conversely, sometimes uncommon or one-of-a-kind items won't garner bidding wars if *nobody* wants them. Let's say you're selling granny's hand-knit toe warmers. The price will likely still remain low, because really, who is going to buy granny's hand-knit toe warmers anyway?

To make an informed assessment of the "going price" for your items on eBay, you need to do a little homework. Take some time to peruse the site, doing keyword searches and browsing the specific categories for other items similar to what you sell. Be sure to do searches of completed items to get the final gavel price on an item, as sometimes bidding will drive the price of hard-to-find items much higher than you might expect. Conversely, items with Buy-It-Now or reserve prices that are too high won't sell at all, and that's not really an accurate picture of the market price for that item.

Prices on eBay fluctuate constantly. That's just the nature of auctions—you can never predict exactly what price your item will sell for. You may end up delighted or you may end up deflated. Buy-It-Now, fixed-price sales, reserve price listing auctions—these different pricing strategies allow sellers to capitalize on the ever-changing marketplace. But even with all these options, the final price of your sale (or whether or not it sells at your fixed price) is still a function of what the eBay market will bear. Keeping a vigilant eye on the going prices for your goods on eBay will help you maximize the amount that you charge for your fixed-priced items, and this will give you a good idea of the prices to expect from auction-style listing sales.

Pricing by Economies of Scale

In addition to cost and demand considerations, you need to factor in "economies of scale." Simply put, economies of scale occur when the cost involved in selling an item decreases with an increase in the quantity sold. This is particularly true for selling multiple quantities of an identical item in either a multiple item listing, fixed-price, or eBay Store listing. The eBay insertion fees for store inventory remain the same whether you're selling a quantity of 1 or 1000, so the larger the quantity listed, the lower your insertion fees will be per unit, thus allowing you to lower your overall price. Selling multiple quantities of a single item allows the seller to spread out the costs of insertion fees and makes additional fee-based enhancements like bold, gallery, and featured listings more affordable on a per-unit basis.

Note: Use this strategy only with products that realize consistent prices on eBay historically. For goods with more "volatile" prices, you could risk losing profit if you saturate the market with too many of them.

Multiple quantity listings also save you time and effort, which reduces your labor costs. It's much quicker to create one item listing, write one item description, and photograph one item to sell a quantity of 100 identical items than it is to create 100 different listings for 100 different items. It's also easier to ship a multiple quantity of identical items with the same box and packaging than to package up many different items in different sized boxes. Conversely, if you sell a variety of individually listed items, you'll need to be sure that your prices are high enough to cover the additional fees and labor-intensive nature of their sale.

The Secret to Pricing Success Is to Test, Test, Test

With these factors in mind, the most important element to creating a pricing strategy for eBay is trial and error, and then tracking your sales results. Test, test, and then test some more. Try selling the same item at a variety of prices to test what the market will bear. Does your sales volume increase if you lower your price? Does the volume increase enough that you profit more than selling it at a higher price? Or would you make more money if you raised the price, but sold less?

If you're going to use a multiple item pricing option for a large quantity of a particular item, run a few trial runs with a single unit at different prices to establish the best price to use when selling a large quantity. Try selling the same item at different times of the year, different days of the week, or even different times of the day. Continue to check other sellers' prices and see how they've priced their items and how quickly their items are selling at those prices. Browse around and see what products are generating the fierce bidding wars in the auction-style format.

Simple Data Tracking

eBay businesses may wish to invest in price-tracking software or even retain the consulting services of pricing strategists. A number of books on pricing strategies for small businesses are available if you want to get really deep into this stuff. However, any eBay business can benefit from gathering data (via simple eBay searches) on the following factors:

* *Number of like items currently for sale versus number of completed items.* This gives you an idea whether the current number for sale is a little or a lot by comparison to previous weeks. It gives you a picture of the current supply on eBay at any given moment and helps you judge current demand for those goods.
* *Prices of your competitors' goods.* Sort your search by highest price first so you get a clear picture of the "ceiling" of the going price of your goods. Also, open some of the high-price listings to examine the title, description, and category. This helps you determine why these listings edged out the competition for higher final prices.
* *Pricing formats used by items garnering highest prices.* Again, examine some of the winning listing auctions and determine whether using an auction-style listing format, Buy It Now, fixed-price, or eBay Store listing is best for your product.
* *Your own sales history, including your total sales, quantity sold, as compared to your cost of selling the products.* This gives you a good idea of your items with high versus low profit margins, as well as best-selling products versus items you may want to discontinue.
* *Price fluctuations and seasonality.* This gives you the larger picture of when to expect maximum demand for different products.

Write down this information, or plug it into a spreadsheet and revisit it frequently. Gathering this data will help you formulate your own customized pricing strategy for each and every product you sell. You'll begin to know intimately the kind of profits you can consistently make on certain items or services. And you'll be able to note deviations (both positive and negative) from your expectations. You'll be able to pinpoint what marketers call "price elasticity," or how your sales volume will shift with increases and decreases in your prices. You'll know when to use an auction-style listing format to maximize bidding and when to sell it quick with an enticing Buy-It-Now price. You'll gain more perspective on seasonality and trends and even days and times when high traffic on eBay yields better sales results. The key is to track your sales and pricing data through both your successes and failures. The process helps you develop a comprehensive understanding of your products' price sensitivity.

Market Research Tools for eBay

Several companies offer powerful tools to assist you with eBay market research. Each compiles data from eBay listings, including most popular items, starting and final bid prices, total sales, and sell-through rates. Information is reported by both category and successful sellers within the category. They also help you predict trends and make wise purchasing, pricing, and positioning decisions for your merchandise. Each service is fee-based, ranging from fairly inexpensive to somewhat pricey. They all are a great way to do your market research homework before jumping in "blind." Here are URLs to a couple of these services:

- **Terapeak Marketplace Research** http://www.terapeak.com/ (readers of this book will receive a 30-day free trial of the powerful researching software; go to http://www.terapeak.com/signup/ Janelle)
- **SmartCollector** http://www.smartcollector.com (for Antiques and Collectibles categories)
- **eBay's Solution Center** http://cgi6.ebay.com/ws/eBayISAPI .dll?SolutionsDirectory

Price and Product Positioning

By understanding some basic product-positioning principles, you can develop pricing strategies for your products. You can employ many different ways to position your product to make it unique in the marketplace. You can employ many different ways to position your product to make it unique in the marketplace, but for the sake of our pricing discussion, let's focus on positioning a product by price.

A high-end pricing strategy positions goods as distinctive and superior, and therefore worthy of a higher price tag. These items are appealing to those who are attracted to a perceived higher value and to the prestige of ownership. Conversely, a low-end pricing strategy positions the product as unique by the nature of its reduced price. To a buyer who loves a bargain, there are no truer words of temptation than "we won't be undersold."

You can even use a mix of low-end and high-end pricing strategies by creating what marketers call *loss leaders*. This strategy prices certain goods at lower-than-market prices to attract customers to a business in the hopes that customers will then purchase higher priced items.

All three of these pricing strategies speak to the emotions and impulses of potential buyers. Use them to maximize your profit and test pricing levels.

Note: Think about your pricing strategy when you're reading the subsequent chapters. It helps you develop other product-positioning decisions, which is a key element to advanced marketing efforts.

In summary, you need to position your product in accordance with your own goals and the needs of the market. You want to pay close attention to profit margins and costs of business, such as sourcing, manufacturing, labor, and operating expenses. You also need to understand how your products are perceived by your existing and prospective customers. This is a key concept central to the next section.

Know Your Customers

Perhaps the most crucial step in understanding your product is evaluating those who will buy it. The cardinal rule in sales, prospecting, and demonstrating is "know your audience" and its relationship to the particular item you're selling. Who are these people that browse your listing or eBay Store? What do they want? A window-shopping experience? The lowest price? The highest quality goods on the market? The best service? The fastest shipping?

To figure all this out, you need to get down to an elemental level and consider who these Web shoppers are. Four basic sets of eyes shop on eBay: browsers, comparison shoppers, prospects, and buyers. We all know the browsers who surf around eBay just for fun and discovery. Comparison shoppers are searching eBay for the best price on an item they need. Prospects know what they're looking for but need to be given a reason to buy it. And buyers, the holy grail, are ready to click that bid button and purchase the item.

Identifying Your Target Market

So how does one go about tipping the scales to turn prospects into buyers? Well, the answer really lies in focusing your efforts on the right type of prospect. Marketing gurus call this process *identifying your target market*. Think about your ideal customer. Sure, the obvious answer is a compulsive shopper with a bottomless bank account. But since that type of person is few and far between, we'll need to get more specific here.

Think about the kind of person who would be interested in your product and describe this person in detail. Consider the buyer's age, sex, profession, income and education levels, and interests or hobbies.

Let's take the example of an eBay seller specializing in Harley Davidson motorcycle parts and gear. There's a very distinct segment of our population who identify themselves as motorcycle enthusiasts, and a subset of those riders who identify themselves with owning and riding a Harley. They spend most of their free time either riding their bikes or fixing them up. Most of these folks have lives that exist well beyond the parameters of the old Hell's Angels stereotype. However, you will note a trend in their demographic: They are mostly aged 35 to 65. Although many women enjoy motorcycles, men generally are more enthusiastic and tend to make the purchasing decisions about motorcycles and gear. There is likely a wide variety of professional backgrounds and income levels in the group; however, the underlying common denominator is that they all choose to spend their discretionary income on their motorcycle hobby. This is a target audience.

Psychographics: The Desires That Drive Your Demographic

Understanding the basic demographic of your target audience will answer the question of *who* will buy your product. But it's equally important to answer the question of *why* they want to buy it. Marketing pros have termed this study *psychographics*. And no, that doesn't mean the trippy liquid projections that Jefferson Airplane used at concerts. Psychographics is a study of likes, dislikes, and the tastes of a demographic group. It addresses the influences on and motivations behind their buying behaviors.

Ask yourself what your customers will find appealing about your product. What sort of need or desire does it fulfill for them? What made them decide to buy your product? Are there any personal values or ideals that play into their purchasing decision?

Ask yourself what your customers will find appealing about your product. What sort of need or desire does it fulfill for them? What made them decide to buy your product? Are there any personal values or ideals that play into their purchasing decision?

To extend the Harley enthusiast example, let's try to journey into the mind of this person. Many motorcyclists would likely describe their motorcycling interest as less of a hobby and more of a lifestyle decision. They cherish the image of traveling down a two-lane highway, dressed in black leather, with the chrome on their bike shining in the bright sun. The bikes reinforce their commitment to ideals like individuality and freedom. Others enjoy being part of the Harley community, where they can express their common interests and be active on the road together. These are all powerful motivators, and you can't afford to ignore them if you're connected to the Harley Davidson market in any way.

You might be thinking that your target audience doesn't seem as well defined as the Harley enthusiast. But if you take the time to address the questions posed in this section, addressing the generalized demographic of your market and their psychographic motivators, you gain more clarity about your target audience. It makes the task of marketing your products so much easier, and your efforts so much more profitable.

A good example of an eBay seller that intimately knows its customer demographic is 2004's Best of Stores winner, The Frenchy Bee. Offering fine products imported from France, this noted seller has zeroed in on the Francophile demographic. The Frenchy Bee understands the desires and demands of their customers, offering elegant and indulgent products that are difficult to find outside of France. They also know that their customers appreciate the French penchant for "beauty for beauty's sake." The Frenchy Bee offers special presentation and packaging of their products, including tissue, ribbons, and small free gifts to their customers. Even their eBay Store design has a French-inspired aesthetic appeal. Figure 1-2 shows The Frenchy Bee eBay Store home page, with specific design elements that appeal to the Francophile demographic.

Figure 1-2 The Frenchy Bee's eBay Store design appeals to the Francophile demographic.

> ### *Seeking New Target Audiences: Thinking Outside the Box*
>
> You may come to realize that you have more than one target market for the same item. Sometimes a little creative thinking about your products and to whom they appeal will reveal new target audiences. Are there segments of the eBay community that you haven't tapped? The secret to this strategy is to brainstorm and test. Think about who else might like your products. Test new waters by putting a few items in front of new audiences. Try out new categories, a variety of keywords, and different positioning approaches. For example, if you're selling black leather boots in the women's shoes category and sales are slow, try adding the word *motorcycle* to the title and putting in the motorcycle category on eBay Motors. Continually revisit and refocus your target market. An entirely new target audience may just fall into your lap.

Motivations and Maslow

Psychographics studies the motivations of your average shopper. Let's think about this concept a little deeper. People purchase goods for a variety of reasons, most of which can be traced back to primal urges like greed, fear, and pleasure. With these fundamental concepts in mind, ask yourself more questions: Is your item going to save people trouble? Will it improve their health or help them avoid certain risks? Will it improve their financial, love, competitive, or practical life? Is it made of chocolate? Will its secret ingredients boost their endorphin levels? Consider the primal, visceral responses and feelings that drive people to make buying decisions.

A study of these basic drives can be taken a bit further, too. Behavioral psychologist Abraham Maslow is credited with classifying motivations beyond the basic primal urges. His findings were useful to a number of fields beyond psychology—most notably (for our purposes), marketing.

He devised his now famous "hierarchy of needs," which includes the following:

- Physiological needs
- The need to feel safe
- The need for love, affection, and a sense of belonging
- The need for esteem
- The need for self-actualization

Many of the ways we connect with customers fall into these hierarchies, and considering that most of us can get enough food and shelter, the categories that go beyond physiological needs become especially important. What many of us want is more of the following:

- Time and efficiency so we can get more food and shelter
- Long-term security
- Protection from psychological fear (real, imminent, or imagined)
- Acceptance into groups
- Approval of family
- Approval of peers and co-workers

We also yearn for self-actualization that lifts our spirits and lends meaning to our livelihoods, day-to-day activities, and relationships.

If we can connect with customers in these areas, then we're really starting to sell. Think about it. Anyone can get a doughnut. But when you get a Krispy Kreme you're getting a special doughnut. Why is it special? Several of Maslow's motivators are at work behind the intense desire for this yummy treat. Of course, it is food, so it does fulfill the physiological need for sustenance. Moreover, Krispy Kreme doughnuts are *comfort* food. Show up at the office with a dozen Krispy Kremes and everybody treats you as if you just walked on water. Your sense of belonging is affirmed. Suddenly, you're the guy who knows good doughnuts, and your need for the esteem and approval of your peers has been fulfilled by some fried dough and sugar glaze.

All this allows Krispy Kreme to charge more for its doughnuts than most other brands. The company has generated demand by paying attention to marketing fundamentals and cultivating a certain mystique around its product. You can do it, too, by paying attention to a few details or going hog wild with a comprehensive, intense marketing plan.

When you start thinking about your products in this way, you're on your way to eBay greatness. Connect with customers at these levels, and soon you'll have a group of customers that shop exclusively with you. It's not necessary to reinvent the wheel here (or in the case of Krispy Kreme, to reinvent the doughnut). What you do need to do is set yourself apart, and you do that by knowing what needs your customers respond to. Know what motivates them.

Whether you're selling an airplane or a chocolate bunny, these motivators are what tip the scales and turn prospects into buyers. They can even turn dedicated low-ball price freaks into consistent, premium-paying customers that swear by your products and service.

A Note About Collectors

No discussion on eBay customers would be complete without addressing the anomaly of the collector. Since the very early days of eBay, collectors have been an integral part of the eBay community. Before the advent of eBay, collectors were forced to limit their hunts to their local geography or the limited areas they traveled, but now they have worldwide access to the objects of their desire. Combine this object accessibility with the feature of a high-speed search engine, and eBay is truly a collector's nirvana.

eBay has also been called a seller's paradise. Dealers of antiques and collectibles used to sit in quiet shops waiting for the right customer to come in, or they'd schlep their goods to trade shows and antiques faires to find buyers. Now, with a few clicks of the mouse, the world of collectors is at their fingertips. And with a broader base of customers, these sellers have more freedom to become specialized in their fields. And best of all, using an auction-style listing format for rare and coveted goods often results in bidding wars that escalate prices beyond their wildest dreams.

Sellers in the collectible fields who grasp the motivations of their customers can reap incredible profits on eBay. Greed, competitiveness, obsession, and fear of "the one that got away" drive collectors to do things that noncollectors probably wouldn't understand. They have a distinct emotional attachment to the items they seek, and they are driven by an intellectual curiosity to research, organize, archive, and preserve these objects. They are very purposeful in their searches and highly competitive in their bidding. They run their favorite keyword searches several times a day. They stalk other collectors' bidding, just in case their own searches missed anything. And they use auction-sniping software to enter last-minute bids, in the hopes of flying under the radar of the bidding competition.

Of course, the bidding phenomenon spans the entire eBay arena. Grown men have been known to fight tooth and nail for such nifty gadgets as global positioning systems. While the average purchaser of a GPS device will likely stop with just one or two (one for him and one for the missus) to fulfill his need to know where he is on the Earth, a "collector" will continue to search eBay for every single GPS make and model manufactured throughout the history of global positioning devices—just for the sake of having them all. There's a saying in the business, "three's a collection," which means that two of anything is usually enough to fulfill any actual *need*; purchase a third and suddenly ownership of this stuff has taken on an entirely different purpose.

The best way for an eBay seller to capitalize on this phenomenon is again to understand the target audience and what it is that causes them to covet the items they collect. Develop an area of expertise, and get to know these items intimately. Research the history of the field and learn as much as you can from other collectors and sellers, discussion boards, reference books, and trade shows. Understand what traits or specific objects are highly desirable to collectors in this field. Learn the language collectors use to describe their collecting field, and figure out the keywords they would use to search for these items. Understand their systems of grading condition and learn to tell the reproductions from the originals. When appropriate, enlist the expertise of independent authentication services to give prospects the confidence to bid on high-ticket items. Effective marketing to collectors does require extra task work and research, but your effort will pay off in good profits and loyal collector customers.

Know Your Competition

After you've analyzed your business, your products, and your customers, you'll want to study your competition closely. We touched on this subject a bit earlier in the chapter, concerning your product and its place in relation to your competitors, their products, and their prices. Now let's take an even more studied look at your competition.

Identify precisely who is your competition—on eBay, on the Internet at large, and in the brick-and-mortar retail world. The perceptions that your customers form concerning your business will be based on a comparison of their experience with your competitors. Closely examine the way your competitors run their businesses. Create a list of five to ten of your closest competitors, and answer the following questions about each one:

- What are their strengths?
- How can you emulate these strengths in your own business?
- What are their weaknesses?
- Does your own business suffer from those same weaknesses?
- What are their pricing structures?
- How is their sales performance?
- What kind of customer service do they offer?

Revisit this list frequently, adding new competitors to the list as they enter eBay. Keeping close track of your competitors helps you identify who is succeeding and why, as well as who is failing and why they're losing ground. It also helps you to recognize your own opportunities for improvement, and you can learn from the mistakes of others, rather than suffer through these errors on your own.

Use Your Competitors' Sales as Your Personal Test Market

Your competitors' sales are an excellent test market for your own products. It's remarkably easier to gather this information from eBay searches than by going to the expense and effort of testing your goods with your own sales. In the brick-and-mortar world, large retailers employ "secret shoppers" whose job it is to go to the competitor's place of business and pretend to be an average customer to study how the competitor is conducting business. Shoppers examine everything from the layout and design of the store, to customer service styles, to merchandise quality and prices, refund policies, and on and on.

Take some time to browse your competitors' listings and eBay Stores. Act as a secret shopper, and be sure to make notes that answer the following questions:

- How do they position their products?
- How do they describe their items?
- How are they differentiating their products?
- Are they presenting goods to customers by paying attention to certain emotional drivers?
- What keywords do they use?
- Under what categories do they list their items?
- Did they use any special features such as bold or featured listing auctions, subtitles, or Gallery pictures?
- What is their level of customer service?
- What shipping options are they offering to their buyers?

The true value in this analysis is to compare these factors with the final outcome of their sales. It gives you a good picture of the effectiveness and profitability of different techniques. You'll get tons of valuable information, without incurring a single insertion fee in the process. We'll discuss how to use this information to maximum advantage in subsequent chapters.

Store Your Searches for Quick Market Research

You can use your My eBay page to store preferences of favorite searches, sellers, and categories. This allows you to store up to 100 of your preferred searches, and you can even set up My eBay to e-mail you when new items match your search criteria. When you add a seller to your favorites, eBay asks if you would like to be e-mailed when the seller lists anything new (a seller's digest). Also, if your competitor has an eBay Store, the favorite seller search will ask if you'd like to be included on the competing store's mailing list. This gives you access to your competitor's marketing mix and retention strategies. You'll also be notified about your competitor's product inventory changes.

In the brick-and-mortar world, it can take weeks, sometimes months, for the marketing/advertising feedback to be returned to the company. On eBay, at a moment's notice, you can see whether your competitors have changed their marketing or their product mix, if they're suddenly offering free shipping, or if they added a hot new item to their listings.

Caution: When browsing your competitors' listings, it can be incredibly tempting to plagiarize an effective item description or "cyber-squat" on someone else's .jpg image of an identical item. Not only is this illegal and strictly forbidden by eBay policy, but it is also incredibly bad karma. Do this and it may come back to haunt you. Instead, take away the solid ideas that seem to be working for your competitors and customize them to work for your own business.

Tie It All Together to Create Your eBay Brand

When you start getting into strategic analysis and planning with respect to your company, your products, your customers, and your competition, you start getting into an area marketing gurus call *branding*. Corporations spend millions to build their brands and devise ways to foster positive consumer perception and confidence. Solid branding strategies bring consumer recognition and loyalty, allowing companies to edge out their competitors and reap huge profits. Companies such as Apple Computer, FedEx, and Southwest Airlines are stellar examples of successful branding strategies, and their customers are positively evangelical in their loyalty. You know what they sell (computers, package delivery, airline flights), but you also know what their brand image is (different/unique, absolutely on time, fun/bargain).

What Is Branding and What Will It Do for My Business?

So what is branding, anyway? Advertising and marketing types have written massive tomes on the subject. We'll try to boil it down to a few key points. Branding is both an effort on the part of the company and a perception felt by customers and prospects. The perception is the key to a brand's success. Your business name, your product, your logo and graphics, a catchy tagline, and your selling style all create perceptions about your brand. At big companies, the way employees answer the phone contributes to brand perception. Customer relations and your reputation for quality and service are perhaps the most important brand influencers. A brand is the fusion of all these factors into a clear and consistent message about your business. It's the feeling people have about your company.

Note: If the Department of Motor Vehicles had a brand it might be described as hellish, with a tagline like "Driving Frustration."

You can think of branding in terms of a promise that tells people what to expect from your business. Of course, the key to any good promise is keeping it. In terms of eBay, this means delivering the product as advertised, communicating with customers, providing top-notch customer service, and standing by your commitments.

Your brand presents your business in the most favorable light and creates demand for your products or services. A consistent brand message

- Lends credibility to your business
- Inspires customer buying confidence
- Generates customer loyalty—marketing's holy grail

Fortunately, you don't need to be a corporate powerhouse to develop your own brand. No matter what your size, you'll gain plenty from even simple branding exercises.

Personify Your Business

A great way to begin building your eBay brand is to think of your business as a person and then describe this person. Describe this person's appearance and clothing. Is the person sophisticated and stylish? Sporty and athletic? Professional and polished?

These qualities will help to determine the visual style of your listings and your store, giving a "face" to your eBay brand. You can dig deeper, too, into issues of personality. Is this person fun and energetic? Innovative and creative? Intelligent and thoughtful? Warm and fuzzy? What about their interests? Do they enjoy technology? Fashion? Music? History? Travel?

You can also explore this person's demeanor and voice. Are they friendly and conversational? Formal and distinguished? Or trendy with the latest street slang? Your company "voice" is an important part of your brand that helps you communicate with your customers. It holds the attention of your target audience in the same way a personable brick-and-mortar salesperson connects with customers.

And how about values? Is the person honest? Hard-working? Environmentally conscientious? Charitable and giving? Concerned with the happiness and satisfaction of others? The values that you establish for your business help build strong customer relations and a solid reputation in the eBay community. Your values also guide the way you interact with your employees and how employees understand your business. From the moment they're hired, they should be learning what your company is all about and how it's supposed to be perceived by the market. And if you create a culture at your workplace where your employees feel valued, they will, in turn, value your customers.

Personify Your Customers

Thinking about your business as a person is a stepping stone to developing the brand of your business fully, but thinking about your customers as a person can be even more valuable. Try to personify your ideal customer. Observe real-life customers at trade shows, trunk shows, or swap meets to get a clearer perception of their personalities. Use all the same questions we've discussed so far and try to get into the head of your customer's personality.

Recap

Can you see how we're coming full circle here? Branding helps us bring all these ideas together—we're pulling together all the major musings of business existentialism.

- Who are you? What is your expertise? What is your niche? What is your mission statement? How does your business name express who you are?
- What are your products? How are they unique and enticing? What kinds of benefits do they provide?

- Who are your customers? What inspires them to buy from you? What can you do to connect with them?
- Who is your competition? How are you different from them? What lessons can you take from them to improve your business?

The subsequent chapters in this book deal with these fundamental issues and themes in much greater detail. This is the jumping off point, however. In case you hadn't noticed, you now have a solid plan. You know what you're selling, how much you're charging, who you're selling to, and what you need to do to build business. All this from some simple introspection and market analysis. Next, we'll get into some specific tools that will help you build your eBay business and market your products.

Chapter 2

Seller's Toolbox: Use eBay and Other Resources to Increase Sales

---

Now that you've taken some time to focus on your business and define your audience, it's time to explore some very tangible resources that will allow you to sell more profitably and efficiently on eBay.

We're not going to go over general eBay mechanics here. Scores of other books devote lots of time to eBay fundamentals. They're full of "click here to do that" sort of advice. Instead, our aim is to assist you in going beyond the basic nuts and bolts of eBay and delve into some more advanced selling tools.

eBay and other third-party services offer some amazing and powerful tools that help you work efficiently, project professionalism, and build profits. However, many sellers don't even know that these tools exist, much less how to utilize them to their fullest potential.

This chapter introduces some of the more advantageous tools and offers some brief how-to instruction. Consider this chapter a toolbox of resources that we'll refer to again and again throughout the book. You'll see specific instances for which the various tools can be applied in strategic marketing contexts. This chapter also includes tips, pointers, and notes about special services and new features on eBay.

Listing Creation and Management Tools

If you're not already using a listing management system, you should be. These tools help you create and manage your listings with efficiency and finesse. They also allow you to automate customer communications and other tedious tasks involved in eBay selling. The time-saving attributes of these tools are fantastic, giving you more time to devote to marketing your products.

eBay's Management Tools

eBay offers some very powerful management tools that help you super-charge your selling. Some PowerSellers use a combination of eBay's Selling Manager Pro along with TurboLister to create and manage a large volume of listings.

Turbo Lister

TurboLister (http://pages.ebay.com/turbo_lister/) is free downloadable software from eBay that enables you to create bulk listings and bulk uploads. It features a single-screen listing form where all the information required for the listing is entered on one page. (Compare this to tediously clicking the Continue button through *seven pages* of the eBay Sell Your Item form.) It also gives you the option of item template customization, bulk listing editing, bulk start time scheduling, and bulk listing uploads. It's truly an incredible timesaver.

> **Note:** Although it's a nifty tool, TurboLister does not work for Mac users. It works only in Windows operating systems.

TurboLister also provides a WYSWIG (what you see is what you get) HTML editor to help you create your listings. It can be used in conjunction with eBay's Listing Designer, which provides HTML templates to help you create attractive and effective listing layouts. Chapter 3 discusses ways to use this tool to create a visual identity that reinforces your eBay business brand.

Selling Manager Pro

Selling Manager Pro is a powerful tool that provides the following features:

- Inventory management functions
- Customer e-mail interfaces with customizable templates
- Payment and shipment tracking
- Bulk printing of invoices and shipping labels
- Custom preferences to automate customer e-mails and feedback
- Sales reporting with profit and loss statements
- Customizable bulk feedback options

You'll note that the word *bulk* appears a couple of times in this list of functions. That's the beauty of this software. Functions such as feedback and customer e-mails that once were handled individually can now be handled dozens at a time. A few simple checks of boxes and clicks of a button and

you're on your way. You can even set preferences to automatically send customers e-mail, notifying them of winning bids, payments received, or items
shipped.

The Selling Manager Pro interface is automatically hosted on your My
eBay page, which gives you access to all your selling activity from any remote
location with Internet access. The interface divides your selling activity into
different views, such as scheduled listings and active listings, that make it
much easier to manage your listings and sales. Figure 2-1 shows Selling Manager Pro as it appears on the My eBay page. Note the variety of views listed
in the left column.

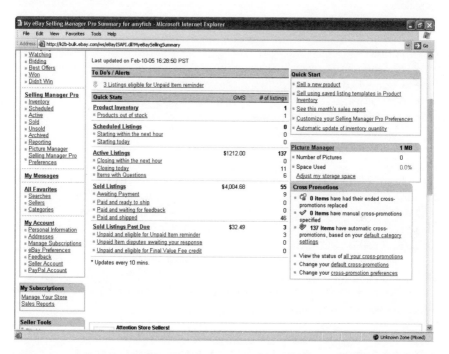

Figure 2-1   Selling Manager Pro is hosted on your My eBay page and offers a variety of
options for sorting and viewing your listings.

Tip: The customizable e-mail templates with Selling Manager Pro offer a
great opportunity for sellers to connect with their customers on a personalized level. This is a powerful tool for creating excellent customer service
and driving repeat customers to your eBay Store. Chapter 6 discusses these
strategies in detail.

An added benefit to using eBay's Selling Manager Pro is that eBay offers
to bundle the cost of this tool with other eBay tools you may already be using.
Although a monthly fee is incurred with Selling Manager Pro (as of this
writing, $15.95 a month), it's offered as a freebie to Featured and Anchor

eBay Stores subscribers. Also, if you choose to use eBay's Listing Designer, with preset HTML templates for listing creation, the usual fees for the service are waived for Selling Manager Pro subscribers.

Third-Party Listing Management Tools

Your options for listing management tools aren't limited to eBay offerings. Literally dozens of companies offer powerful tools and services that interface with eBay and provide functions similar to Turbo Lister and Selling Manager Pro. The following are a few of the most commonly used by PowerSellers:

- **Mpire**   http://www.Mpire.com (Mpire offers users a free 30-day trial period)
- **Kyozou**   http://www.kyozou.com/next_gen.html
- **ChannelAdvisor**   http://www.channeladvisor.com
- **Marketworks**   http://www.marketworks.com
- **Auction Hawk**   http://www.auctionhawk.com
- **Vendio**   http://www.vendio.com
- **Auction Sage**   http://www.auctionsagesoftware.com

Some of these tools operate in a more limited capacity but come at a less expensive price than eBay's tools. Others offer a higher level of functionality and can be customized to accommodate your particular business. Of course, these types of services are more costly, but if you're selling at a high rate and volume, it can be worth the investment.

Do your homework and investigate which selling creation and management tool is right for your business. You'll find a great overview of these services, along with their pricing structure and links to each service's Web site, at http://www.auctionbytes.com/cab/pages/ams.

Other Cool Tools to Help List and Manage Sales

While listing and selling management tools will be your best friends, quite a few other tools deserve to be included in your clique. Some are experimental and as yet unproven, and others just make a whole lot of practical sense. eBay's Best Offer and the Infopia Configurator, for example, promise to have a direct effect on sales. Picture editors and hosting tools help make your listings look good and load fast. That's marketing, to some extent— merchandising, really. Fee calculators, shipping tools, and international selling tools are also covered in this section.

Bid Negotiation Tool

eBay's Best Offer is a new tool that gives buyers and sellers the ability to negotiate prices on Fixed Price and Store Inventory format listings. The seller has to designate the Best Offer option in the listing, and the buyer has to find them within Buy-It-Now items. (Buyers need to be in the View Item listing page to see whether Best Offer is available.) A special text message box is available (up to 500 characters allowed), where viewers can propose a lower or higher bid and offer an explanation. Sellers have the option to accept or decline (or ignore) any offers made. The service is free to both parties.

The offers and their acceptances are considered binding by eBay, just as a bid is. The final accepted Best Offer price is subject to eBay Final Value Fees. All the details are described at http://pages.ebay.com/bestoffer/faq/index.html.

Note: Since Best Offer is a new tool, we've yet to see how it's going to perform. If buyers are willing to consider the fair market value of the goods, it could prove to be a great tool that offers choice and empowerment to buyers, resulting in bigger bottom lines for sellers. On the other hand, it could end up being a nightmare for sellers who spend too much time fielding "low-ball" bids from stingy buyers. Time will tell.

Custom Product Configuration

Infopia's Configurator (http://www.infopia.com/products/configurator.shtml) helps sellers offer buyers a way to create their own customized items (think computers with different components, or different sizes and colors for clothing and shoes). Dell and Nike offer the most high-profile examples of how this works outside of eBay. You can get any kind of custom computer from Dell by clicking through the company's Web site, and Nike allows you to design your own shoes on its site.

For eBay, Configurator allows the seller to create one listing with a variety of item options at different price points. The buyer clicks the options she wants and Configurator automatically generates a Buy-It-Now listing with the price adjusted according to the customer's selections.

The Configurator encourages buying behavior by empowering buyers to make their own choices and involving them in a personal shopping process. Configurator also has the potential to save sellers a lot of money in listing fees since only one item listing needs to be created with the Configurator. This gives sellers more money to invest in fancy upgrades like Home Page Featured to gain maximum exposure. This is a prime example of demand-driven commerce—with minimal effort and expense on your part and happy customers who have chosen the exact product they want. Figure 2-2 shows an example of the Configurator in action.

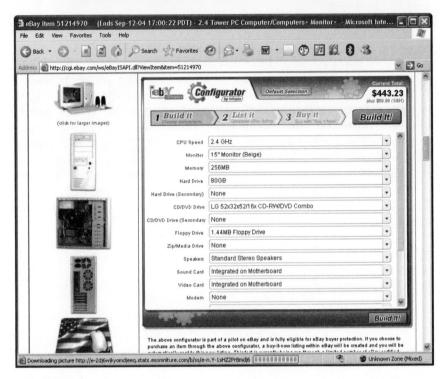

Figure 2-2 This sample eBay Listing uses the Configurator interface, allowing buyers to build their own computer with different components at different prices.

eBay Picture Manager

Although it might seem like a brainless chore, image management and hosting is actually marketing-critical. It's essentially a merchandising issue: If your pictures don't load fast and present accurately, you've got a problem. Any delay in loading time offers the window shopper an opportunity to click away, and poorly presented images make your offerings look unprofessional and uninviting. If you're limiting the number of photos you use with a listing due to the cost of adding extra images, you're missing a huge opportunity for changing browsers into bidders.

With eBay's Picture Manager, you can upload pictures for eBay to host and easily manage them from the Sell Your Item form, My eBay, the Selling Manager tools, and eBay Stores. The service enables bulk picture uploads, and you can add multiple pictures to listings without paying extra fees. Adding, deleting, and organizing your pictures from within eBay is a big time saver, but the cost can be prohibitive for some sellers. The pricing runs from no charge to $39.99 (as of this printing), based on the number of megabytes you upload. It may be cheaper than paying eBay for each and every extra image you add to your listing. More information is available at http://pages .ebay.com/picture_manager/manager.html.

Smart Image Hosting

If you want to maximize your dough, use your own Web hosting to host your eBay photos or use a third-party image manager such as inkFrog, Village Photos, or Photobucket. Many of the third-party listing management services offer image hosting as part of their packages, too.

Your own Web hosting may consist of a site you already have up or some space your ISP offers for free. Just create a folder dedicated to your eBay images, upload your photos to it, and then link to the images in that folder through your eBay auctions.

Consider how much storage space and bandwidth you need before committing to one of these options. Examine the number of listings you have, how many pictures you use in each and how many hits your listings get. The more hits you receive, the more bandwidth you'll need. For example, if you run 100 to 150 listings with an average of three images each, an adequate amount would be 25MB of storage and 1GB of monthly bandwidth (assuming the images are of reasonable file size—under 50K each).

Tip: Shop around. Image hosting is one area where you can really reduce costs while improving the performance of your eBay listing pages.

Image-Editing Software and Services

If you're already using software such as Adobe Photoshop to edit your eBay images, that's great. Photoshop is the *crème de la crème,* and you already know it. However, if Photoshop is beyond your budget or computer skill level, you can use a few other tools that aren't quite as expensive and can still get the job done for Web purposes.

Pixby Software's Fast Photos tool (http://www.pixby.com) is specifically designed for online auction sellers. It features automatic size optimization, gallery creation, watermarking, professional borders and drop shadows, as well as all the usual resizing, sharpening, and enhancement tools.

Other products with similar features include the following:

- **IrfanView**   http://www.irfanview.com
- **Photoshop Elements**   http://www.adobe.com/products
- **Paint Shop Pro**   http://www.jasc.com/products/paintshoppro
- **Microsoft Picture It! Premium**   http://www.microsoft.com/products/ imaging
- **FotoKiss**   http://www.fotokiss.com

- **PhotoImpression** http://www.arcsoft.com/en/products/photoimpression
- **FotoFinish** http://www.fotofinish.com

All of these software products have free trial downloads, so you can work with them before plunking down your money. Ultimately, you'll stick with the editor that you feel most comfortable with. Certain interfaces and processes just feel right for different people.

Note: We discuss photography and image-editing tips and tricks in Chapter 3.

eBay Fee Calculators

Fee calculators are great for several reasons: They help you price items, evaluate bidding expectations, and decide which listing upgrades to consider. Here are two good products to check out:

- **FeeFinder** http://www.hammertap.com/FeeFinder.html
- **eMarket Manager's fee calculator** http://www.emarketmanager.com

When you know exactly how much you'll incur in eBay fees, you can price your listings more accurately. These calculators let you plug in scenarios of final bid price to calculate final value fees. You can also calculate item cost and shipping and handling costs to get a total picture of profit on any given item.

Escape the Post Office

Please tell us that you'll never wait in a post office line again. Please. With the print-your-own USPS and UPS services available directly through your My eBay page or third-party postage services such as Endicia.com and Stamps .com, there's just no need to wait. You can also set up merchant accounts with Pitney Bowes, UPS, FedEx, or DHL. All of these tools and accounts offer plenty of options to help you automate shipping processes, create professional-looking labels, and save huge amounts of time.

Internationalism

Selling internationally does come with certain risks: payment and shipping can be tricky and not quite as secure as domestic transactions. However, it's also full of sales potential. When the US dollar is weak, foreign shoppers enjoy extra buying power on eBay, and they tend to spend like crazy. International sales are booming—so get on board!

Here are a couple of nifty tools to make international selling easier.

BorderFree.com

This customs clearance/shipping center site processes international payments and forwards the money directly to you. It also gives you a "ship to" address of the company's warehouse in the United States, from which your package is sent to its international destination.

Google Language Tools

These tools, located on the Google home page, help you overcome language barriers with a simple cut and paste. Just place text into the box, select the language To and From information, and the text is translated into your or your customer's language. It works best if you keep your text simple—use very basic sentence construction and simple words for accurate translation. Your international customers and prospects will really appreciate this.

eBay Stores

eBay Stores offer easy-to-establish channels for marketing goods and growing your eBay business. The all-in-one eBay Store package makes it easy to create your own online selling presence, even if you have no previous Web design experience.

You get your own customizable URL address, where buyers can link directly to your professional-looking eBay Store. Store subscriptions also include your own search engine that allows customers to search items in your store only, keeping them shopping with you rather than clicking over to other sellers.

Your store is also listed in eBay's Store Directory—a sort of yellow pages for eBay buyers to find store sellers and their goods. eBay automatically submits your store's information to Internet search engines such as MSN, Google, and Yahoo!, which helps to drive buyers to your store from outside of eBay.

Every store subscription comes with powerful sales and traffic reporting as well as new promotional and cross-selling tools. Best of all, listing fees for fixed-price store inventory literally cost just pennies, creating potential for larger profit margins than regular eBay listings.

Opening an eBay Store or Improving Your Existing One

Opening an eBay Store is quick and easy. We'll walk you through the process here. If you already have an eBay Store, read through this section anyway. eBay recently added several new features and options to help you customize your store, and this section will help you maximize your selling potential.

Note: At the outset of this chapter, we stated that we would shy away from nuts-and-bolts type instruction. However, because the eBay Store is an integral part of any eBay marketing strategy, yet so many eBay sellers don't take advantage of its potential, we offer an in-depth discussion of eBay Stores here. We'll be referring to eBay Stores frequently in the other chapters also, so this section contains important reading.

Select Your Subscription Level

The first thing you'll need to do is make a decision about what eBay Store subscription level is right for you. There are three levels to choose from: Basic, Featured, and Anchor Stores. Each comes with its own particular benefits. For more information on the fees and benefits to the different eBay Stores subscription levels, go to http://pages.ebay.com/storefronts/Subscriptions .html.

Featured and Anchor Stores come with additional perks at a higher price tag:

- Additional custom store pages
- Additional e-mail marketing capabilities
- Expanded traffic and stores reporting
- Monthly allotments of free keyword advertising

These additional perks and features will be explained in greater detail as we progress through this section.

Tip: For medium-sized sellers who also use Selling Manager Pro, the Featured Store subscription represents the best value, as your Selling Manager Pro subscription fees are included in your monthly store subscription fee, along with a $30 credit toward the eBay Keywords program (explained later in the chapter). Individually, these value-added services total more than the monthly fee for a Feature Store subscription.

Open or Change Your Store

If you don't already have an eBay Store, you'll need to set up a few basic elements. Go to the eBay home page and click the eBay Stores link from the left menu, or go to http://Stores.ebay.com/. This links you to the eBay Stores main page. Click the blue Open A Store button in the upper-right corner to begin the process of opening your store.

Note that any settings you create when first opening your eBay Store can be edited at any time. You can upgrade or downgrade your subscription level whenever you wish, too. Sellers who already have an eBay Store and wish to revise their store setup can click the Manage My Store button (upper right) to link to their store management page. Figure 2-3 shows a view of the

Figure 2-3   eBay Stores main page

eBay Stores main page. Here, you'll find an eBay Stores directory, with Anchor level store logos displayed at the top. Featured level stores are listed below. All stores are listed by category and alphabetically with links to the left. The links to open or manage your store are located at the upper right. (Note also the visibility of the Anchor Stores logos in the Stores Directory.)

Choose a Store Design

Click the Open A Store button. You'll begin by choosing a store design. You can use one of eBay's 39 predesigned store templates or use the eBay Easily Customizable tool (click the link in the upper-left corner of the page) to create a customized store look. We suggest choosing the Classic Left or Classic Top templates. These templates allow you to customize the appearance of your store, which is an excellent opportunity to build on your business's identity and brand. We further discuss brand-building store design strategies in Chapter 3.

The Classic Left and Classic Top templates are also a wise choice for optimizing your store for search engines. These templates display the keywords of your store's name and description (which we'll discuss in the following two sections) at the top of your store pages. This is an important element to making your store pages visible to search engines. eBay studies have shown that the search engines will not be able to "spider" words that are covered up by the template. Classic Left and Classic Top allow your Store Name and Store Description to show through.

Choose a Store Name

After you've chosen a basic store design, you'll be prompted to choose your eBay Store name. Give your store name special attention; although it's just 35 characters in length, those 35 characters are critical for search engine optimization. Your store name is one of the keyword text elements that are submitted by eBay to Internet search engines, so the name you give your store should reflect the products you sell. That way, buyers searching the Internet for your specific product are more likely to find your eBay Store.

For instance, your business name and eBay user ID could be Jean's Fine Quilts. Your eBay Store, however, could be named something like Quilt Patterns Fabrics Notions Sew—this way, the store name is filled with keywords so it will be easily spotted by people searching the Internet for quilts, patterns, fabrics, and similar sewing-related items. Then, once the user sees your listing on her search results and clicks the link, she'll go to your store and see your business name, branding, and goods for sale.

Write a Store Description

The next store section to set up is the 300-character store description. Your store description is another area in which the text is submitted by eBay to Internet search engines, so again, choose your words carefully. This is not the place to say, "Hi. Welcome to our store. Please feel free to browse." While that's certainly a kind greeting, it doesn't contain a single word that a potential buyer would use to search for the goods you sell. It's better to be highly descriptive of what you sell, including specific products and brand names.

Some sellers use this space to list their goods—creating store descriptions such as KitchenAid blender, Senseo coffee maker, Black & Decker juicer—until they reach their 300-character maximum. While this truly optimizes the searchability of the eBay Store, some might fear they're losing an opportunity to connect with the buyer on a more emotional level. In the following section on customizing your store, we'll share a tip on using a customized store header to create a warm-and-fuzzy greeting to your customers.

Insert a Logo

The final step in setting up your eBay Store is to insert your logo. You'll notice in this section that eBay offers predesigned logos along with the option to insert your own logo. We strongly suggest you avoid using the predesigned logos. These designs are generic and do nothing to assert your particular business's identity or individuality.

Having a personalized logo allows you to look professional while maintaining a consistent branding theme throughout all aspects of your eBay business. Chapter 3 discusses logo design at length and shows you simple methods for creating your own stylish and professional logo.

Tip: Avoid using the predesigned logos provided by eBay. Buyers immediately recognize these as eBay stock images and they do not express your business's individuality or brand identity.

Customizing Your eBay Store

After your basic store setup is complete, you can go about customizing your store for maximum customer impact and Internet searchability. To create your custom settings, open your eBay Store page, scroll down to the bottom, and click the Seller, Manage Store hotspot in the lower-right corner. This links you to your Manage Your Store page, which is command central for your eBay Store. Let's get started.

Store Design Tab

On the left menu of your Manage Your Store page, you'll see a link to Store Design. Click this link if you want to edit any of your basic setup items, such as your name, description, logo, or store theme and appearance. You can also select the way you want your items to be displayed (by gallery picture or by text list) and the order in which you want them to be shown (ending first, highest price, and so on). For subscribers to Featured and Anchor Stores, you can also choose the style of the eBay header on your store from the Store Design page. Finally, the Store Design page gives you links to set your custom categories and pages, which we describe next. Figure 2-4 shows a sample of the eBay Store Design page.

Set Your Custom Categories

Custom categories are a great way to organize your inventory so buyers can easily navigate your store and find the merchandise they seek. You can create 19 custom categories—and eBay sets the twentieth as "Other" by default. Choose your categories carefully, and be sure they make logical sense to your customers. The words you use as custom category titles are also among the text that eBay submits to search engines, so choose category titles that are searchable. For instance, rather than choosing the word *kit* as a category, you could choose a string of more searchable words like *Shelby Cobra model kit cars*. Going this route would also utilize all 29 characters for search engine optimization.

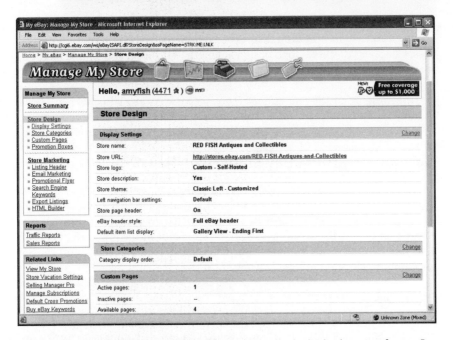

Figure 2-4 On the eBay Store Design page, you can edit the basic elements of your eBay Store, including your name, description, logo, and more.

After you've set up your categories, every listing you create will offer the option of choosing two different store categories to host the listing in your store. This allows you to be very specific with your store categories without having to pigeonhole your listings into any one category.

eBay also gives you the power to change the display order of your custom categories on the left navigation bar. (From your Manage Your Store Page, click Store Categories from the left menu, and use the up and down arrows to re-order your categories). This allows you to feature certain categories and quickly adapt your promotions to a fast-changing market.

Create a Custom Listing Header

Your custom listing header, once created and activated, appears at the top of every listing you create on eBay. It's a great way to drive traffic to your eBay Store and create a brand presence on all of your eBay listings.

To create a custom listing header, click the Listing Header button from the left menu on the Manage Your Store page and activate the Show My Custom Listing Header In My Listings option. By default, the header will include your store name, a link to your store, and the thematic colors you have chosen for your store, as shown in Figure 2-5. You may also include your logo and

Figure 2-5 This Custom Listing Header features the seller's logo, a search box for goods in their eBay Store, and links to specific custom categories.

a store search box for only your listings. In addition, you can include up to five links to your store, which can be any of the custom categories or custom pages that we describe in the next section. Preview your header, and then click the Save Settings button, and your custom listing header is automatically added to all existing and future listings.

Create a Custom Store Page Header

We mentioned previously that your store's description field is not the best place to offer a greeting to your customers. Because the limited 300-character space is essential for search engine optimization, it's crucial to fill this field with searchable keywords that will help browsers find your store and your goods. However, if you wish to offer a greeting that connects with the viewer on a more emotional level, we suggest creating a custom Store Page Header.

You can add either regular text or HTML to the header of your store, which gives you the option of including additional images, navigational links, special item showcases, or messages to your customers. The content you add by customizing your store header will appear at the top of all your store pages.

To customize your store header:

1. Go to the Manage Your Store page.
2. Click Display Settings from the left menu.
3. Scroll down and click Change in the Store Header Display section.
4. Activate the "Yes, include additional information in the header" button.
5. Enter your text or HTML in the window provided.
6. Click Save Settings.

Create Custom Pages

Depending on your subscription level, you also have the ability to create 5, 10, or 15 custom pages for your eBay Store. These unique pages can be used for a variety of purposes, such as explaining your store policies, detailing special deals and promotions, highlighting specific merchandise, or offering a history of your business. You can even set your existing eBay About Me page to be a custom page in your eBay Store.

Creating custom pages is easy:

1. From your Manage Your Store page, click Custom Pages from the left menu.
2. Click the Create new page button.
3. Use the design wizard to create your page with your choice of seven preformatted templates, or use an eighth custom HTML page to insert your own design.
4. Set the order appearance of your custom pages on the navigation bar of your store by clicking the Move Page arrows.
5. Use the Deactivate option to store a custom page for future use. This is especially helpful for managing special promotions or alternating the content of your eBay Store to keep it fresh and interesting for your customers.

Macromedia Contribute 3 for eBay Stores Development

Macromedia, the Web design software company, developed a version of its Contribute 3 software that interfaces with eBay Stores. This tool provides professional-level Web-building tools along with hundreds of HTML templates to take your eBay Store design to the next level.

Sellers with limited computer skills might find the software a bit difficult to navigate. However, sellers with moderate to good computer skills can use Contribute 3 as a viable alternative to hiring a professional to customize their store design. More information is available at http://www.macromedia.com/software/contribute/special/ct3_ebay. If you already own the current version of Macromedia Contribute 3, the eBay Store extension can be downloaded for free from the same Web address.

Create Listings for Your eBay Store

After your eBay Store is created, your existing auction-format and regular fixed-price listings are automatically inserted into your store. The beauty of eBay Stores, however, is that you can also list merchandise as fixed-price store inventory with incredibly cheap listing fees: just 3 cents for a month-long listing (2 cents for the listing and an extra penny gets you a gallery picture). Once your store is set up, you're automatically given the option to create a store listing in the listing format section of the eBay sell form. (We discuss store and auction cross-pollination strategies in Chapter 5.)

> **Note:** The Final Value Fees that eBay charges for sales from your store listings are slightly higher than the Final Value Fees for auctions, Buy-It-Now, and regular fixed-price format listings. Even with this higher Final Value Fee, the value for store listings still holds great profit potential. For more information on the stores fee structure, go to http://pages.ebay.com/Storefronts/pricing.html.

Another benefit of store inventory is longer durations for your listings. Choose from 30-, 60-, 90-, or 120-day listings, or choose the GTC (Good 'Til Cancelled) option, which automatically relists your merchandise in 30-day increments until it sells (or until you cancel the listing). Automating this listing function can be a terrific time-saver.

An extra perk to the eBay Store listing is that you can list multiple quantities or SKUs for the same price as listing just one item. With regular eBay listings, your Insertion fees are multiplied by the total quantity offered for sale. With the store listings, you can list up to 10,000 units of a single item—all for just 3 cents a month. Do the math: This has incredible potential to save you a bundle in listing fees. Used with the GTC feature, your listing will automatically renew until all of the quantity has been sold.

Core eBay Searches and Store Listings

One major caveat to the cheap listing fees and longer durations is that store listings do not appear in general keyword searches of the eBay site. However, when a search results in less than 20 items from regular eBay listings, eBay will add to the general search results up to 30 listings from various eBay Stores.

To avoid these or similar problems associated with searches, you'll need to drive traffic to your eBay Store. Driving buyers to your eBay Store is the key factor in your store's success and profitability.

Driving Traffic to Your eBay Store

It is not enough just to open an eBay Store, stock it with merchandise, and then sit back and hope that your merchandise sells. You have to promote, promote, and then promote some more. Fortunately, you can use a few tips, tricks, and tools to make this easy.

Cross-Promotions

eBay provides every store subscriber with cross-promotion boxes that display up to 12 additional items you currently have for sale. (Items are pictured four-at-a-time in the display box with a scroll bar for viewers to use to see additional items.) This box encourages interested buyers to browse your other listings and can increase your sales dramatically. It's added automatically to every item listing page, as well as the bid confirmation and purchase confirmation pages that your customers view when they make a purchase. Figure 2-6 shows a sample of the eBay cross-promotion box.

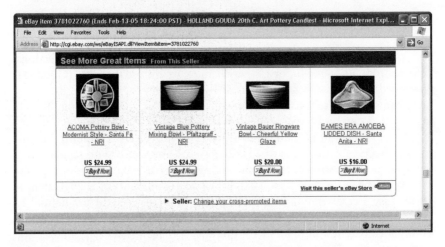

Figure 2-6   The cross-promotion box is automatically added to every listing created by eBay Stores subscribers.

The cross-promotion tool can be customized in a variety of ways. Chapter 5 discusses ways to use this tool to increase its promotional and sales potential.

> **Tip:** By default, the cross-promotion box appears with a yellow border. However, you can customize the appearance of your cross-promotion box to match the branded color theme of your eBay Store. From your Manage Your Store page, click the Customize Cross-Promotion display link to change your settings.

Promotional Boxes

eBay offers store sellers the ability to create customized promotional boxes. These are easy to create and work well for featuring a new product or advertising specials such as free shipping promotions or blowout sales. However, if you have more than one eBay Store (many eBayers do this to sell in different niche markets), you can also use the promotional boxes to link buyers to your other eBay Stores.

Promotional boxes are the perfect marketing feature for cross-promoting all of your eBay businesses in each of your stores. You can create these boxes to show up in your store header and/or in the left-hand navigational toolbar. Just like the store templates, promotional boxes can be as simple as you want or as complex as you choose to make them. They can include graphics, clickable links, custom colors, and text.

To create your own promotional box, click the link for Promotion Boxes from the left menu of your Manage Your Store page.

E-mail Marketing

eBay has created an e-mail marketing program to help drive traffic to your eBay Store. This program is fully integrated with your eBay Store, and it's quick and easy to set up. Chapter 6 discusses how to use the e-mail marketing program and incorporate it in a larger customer retention strategy to build your business. More information is also available at http://pages.ebay .com/storefronts/emailmarketing.html.

Customize Keywords for Meta Tags

You've already learned that eBay submits the text from your eBay Store name, description, and category titles to search engines. Another way eBay helps with search engine optimization is through meta tags. Meta tags are "invisible" text code that are crawled by search engines but not seen on your Web pages. (If you want to view this code, open any of your eBay Store pages, right-click, and select View Source. A new window will open, showing a slough of technical programming code—the first several lines you see are the meta tags of the page being viewed.)

eBay creates these meta tags by default, pulling text from your store name, description, custom category names, and titles of your item listings. However, you can customize the keywords that eBay uses to create your store's meta tags. To do so, click Search Engine Keywords from the left menu on the Manage Your Store page.

When you enter this field, you'll see that each custom page of your store has its own set of keywords—divided into primary and secondary keywords. We recommend that you keep your primary keywords set to the defaults of your eBay Store name and custom categories, because this is the text that will be shown in boldface on search result listings. (If you think that your store name is not searchable enough, you could change the primary keywords for better search results without having to rename your store.)

Revise the secondary keywords to focus on terms buyers are most likely to use to find your goods. Remove extraneous words such as *and* or other words not likely to be searched. Consider related keywords and synonyms, and avoid using the same terms repeatedly. Once you've reset your keywords, preview the page and right-click View Source again to confirm that your new meta tags are more appropriate for the page.

Tools to Help with Keyword Selection

To assist with your keyword selection, try using one or several of the following tools that provide keyword search frequency, recommendations for associated keywords, and the keywords that are seeing the hottest action:

- **Overture Free Search Tool** http://inventory.overture.com/
- **Google AdWords Keyword Tool** https://adwords.google.com/select/main?cmd=KeywordSandbox
- **Lycos Top 50** http://50.lycos.com/

eBay also gives you the most popular keyword searches, organized by category. Go to http://www.ebay.com/sellercentral, click on What's Hot, and then click on Hot Items By Category. This tells you which categories are "hot," meaning that they receive more bids and higher final prices than other categories. You can also go to the same Web site and click on Category Tips. Click on In Demand under the category in which you are selling to find the top search words. Also, http://pulse.ebay.com/ allows you to find the top search words for any of the 52,000 categories on eBay.

> **Tip:** Keywords and meta tags are just two of many ways that search engines rank their results. Higher search result ranking also comes from factors such as the number of inbound links (the more the better) and "stickiness" (how long users stay and browse) for any given Web page. For more information about how search engines work and ways to optimize your store's searchability, go to http://www.searchengines.com. It explains the ways that search engines work in clear, understandable terms.

Register Your eBay Store Name as a Domain Name

If you don't have an existing Web site, consider registering your eBay Store name as a domain name on the Internet. Even if you don't build your own Web site right away, you can still set the domain to redirect browsers automatically to your eBay Store. Although you can register your domain name with any Web-hosting company, eBay has partnered with several companies to help you with this process. As part of their domain registration, these companies offer services such as automatically setting up your redirect to your eBay Store. For a link to these services, go to your Manage Your Store page and Click Domain Registration from the left menu.

Registering your domain helps ensure that if and when the time comes to create your own Web site, the domain name of your choosing will be available. You will also have a built-in base of customers who have already bookmarked your URL.

Note: If your business name is longer than a couple of short words or could be difficult to spell, it makes sense to get two domain names: one reflecting your exact store name, and a second one with a shortened version of the store name that will be easier for customers to remember. Both domains can be set up to redirect to your store. Companies such as Hewlett-Packard use this technique so that those typing in their full name as the URL will find their site (http://www.hewlett-packard.com), as well as those who know the shortcut (http://www.hp.com).

Use Regular eBay Listings to Drive Traffic to Your Store

Once your store is up, running, and full of Store inventory listings, you can use some of the more expensive eBay auction-format listings as a means of advertising and propelling customers to your eBay Store. With the auction-format listings, your goods will come up in core eBay searches, and once your customers have found you, they'll be provided with plenty of clickable links to enter your eBay Store (including the custom listing header discussed earlier). Naturally, you'll want to continue to use auction-format listings for scarce goods that have the potential for bidding wars. But for goods with predicable prices, you can all but abandon the regular format listing except to drive traffic to your eBay Store. Chapter 5 discusses this strategy further and gives you HTML codes to create clickable links.

Tip: Use the 10-day listing option for your listings that you create to promote your store goods. For an extra 40 cents, you'll get three more days of eBay core search visibility.

Place Your Store URL Everywhere

Include your store URL anywhere and everywhere you can. You can create potential for new customers in even the most unlikely places. Add it to every e-mail you send out—Chapter 6 discusses customizing e-mail templates and creating e-mail signatures that include your URL. Include it on every invoice and on every package you send out. Stamp it on your bills or your kids' homework, print it on t-shirts, or put it on the side of your car. Saturate the world with your URL. You never know who will see it.

eBay Stores Reporting Features

The final perk to an eBay Store is the complimentary reporting tools provided to store subscribers. These include basic and advanced traffic reporting tools, as well as accounting tools that export reports directly to Intuit QuickBooks accounting software.

Traffic Reporting

Offered free to all store subscription levels, the traffic report is a powerful reporting tool available on the Manage Your Store page. It's offered through an eBay partner, Omniture, so you'll need to sign Omniture's user agreement to access the report. The report provides information about traffic to all pages in your eBay Store, including all item listings (in any format) and all custom pages in your store.

The traffic report tells you what days of the week see the heaviest customer traffic, which pages were visited most often, and which outside Web sites and search words brought visitors to those pages. This information can help you determine the best days and times to start and end your auction –format listings. It can help you focus in on the most effective keywords for your goods.

Featured and Anchor Store subscriptions are privy to advanced reporting functions like Path Reports and Bidding & Buying Reports:

- **Path Reports**   Show how buyers enter your store, and the progression of pages they click when they browse your store. It also reports at which page they exit your store. This will help you determine whether you need to adjust the custom pages to keep your buyers lingering longer and purchasing more goods.
- **Bidding & Buying Reports**   Delve deeper into how your buyers are responding to your listings. These reports measure listing success rates and which keywords led to the most bidding and sales.

Sales Reports Plus

This cool little sales reporting tool is offered free to eBay Stores subscribers (a $4.99 per month value). The report includes the following information:

- Total sales
- Your successful listings
- Average sale price
- Detailed summary of eBay and PayPal fees and credits
- Sales by category
- Sales by selling format
- Sales by ending time, ending day, and listing duration
- Unpaid item activity

Use the information from Sales Reports Plus to help make wise decisions about the merchandise you carry (and merchandise that should be discontinued), product positioning and pricing, the best listing formats for different goods, and the best times to end your auctions to maximize bidding activity.

Featured and Anchor Store subscribers are given the added reporting benefit of comparing their own sales data with that of the general eBay marketplace sales statistics for the categories in which they sell. This is important information to help you benchmark your own success against that of your competitors.

eBay Accounting Assistant

eBay also offers a free service to eBay Stores and Selling Manager Pro subscribers that allows you to export your sales data directly to QuickBooks accounting software. Designed to work seamlessly, even with existing QuickBooks setups, this handy tool can save you tons of time doing data entry for your bookkeeping. For more information, go to http://pages.ebay.com/ accountingassistant/.

Other Marketing, Promotion, and Customer Service Tools

A few extra tools should be mentioned that help you save money on your operational costs, boost your sales, and cement your status as a reputable eBay seller. They include the eBay Stores Referral Credit program, eBay Keyword Campaigns, and SquareTrade. Lastly, if you operate a Web site outside of eBay, we will discuss a few nifty services that help you integrate your eBay sales with your other e-commerce ventures.

eBay Stores Referral Credit

eBay Store subscribers have the opportunity to qualify for 75 percent off the Final Value Fees for sales from their store inventory for promoting their store outside of eBay. The Store Referral Credit is applied when buyers link directly to your eBay Store or a specific store listing from outside eBay and purchase the item. This is where it quite literally pays to promote your eBay Store through direct e-mail marketing efforts and plastering your URL everywhere. Your search engine optimization efforts that bring customers to your eBay Store from Google, Yahoo!, and other search engines will also yield 75 percent off the Final Value Fees for resulting store inventory sales. For more information on maximizing your Final Value Fees savings through this program, visit http://pages.ebay.com/help/specialtysites/referral-credit-faq.html.

Tip: Remember the earlier suggestion to register your domain name and automatically redirect your traffic to your eBay Store? Sales resulting from those redirects qualify for the Store Referral Credit, too.

eBay Keywords

The eBay Keywords program helps you market your products specifically to those who are searching for your goods on eBay. Who better to focus your advertising efforts than someone seeking the exact product you sell? You can also use the eBay Keywords program for general advertisement of your eBay Store.

The program creates banner ads or text boxes that appear at the top of the screen above the search results for any given keyword search on eBay. Sellers set their own cost-per-click (CPC) pricing and pay only when a browser clicks their banner or text box advertisement. The ads are placed in a rotating order—sellers who set the highest CPC prices receive priority visibility and increased frequency of their ads.

The program also provides keyword management tools that allow sellers to create their own keyword campaigns with a variety of keywords associated with a certain product. These tools also help sellers track the success of campaigns and manage keyword budgets.

Note: eBay Featured and Anchor Stores subscribers receive a monthly budget to spend on Keywords campaigns as part of their monthly eBay Stores fees. As of this writing, featured subscribers receive $30 and Anchor Stores receive $100 toward the Keywords program each month. This is essentially *free* advertising money; use it to your advantage!

A complete explanation of the eBay Keywords program is available at http://www.ebaykeywords.com.

Tip: Although eBay spends a great deal of money buying keywords for their sellers, you can take it a step further by buying your own pay-per-click ad words on Google, Yahoo!, MSN, and other search engines. These operate similarly to the eBay Keywords program. Although more expensive, they reach well beyond the parameters of eBay-only searches and can bring new customers to your eBay Store. The added bonus of buying your own ad words is that browsers link directly to your eBay Store, instead of to a list of eBay search results that also includes your competitors' goods.

SquareTrade

SquareTrade is an independent seller verification and dispute mediation provider used by many trusted eBay sellers. By enrolling in the SquareTrade program, sellers agree to maintain a high standard of selling practices, including fair pricing, accurate item descriptions, and honorable customer service policies. They also submit for verification their identity, business name, and business address. In exchange, they may display the SquareTrade seal on their eBay listings, indicating to potential buyers that they are worthy of trust.

SquareTrade also assists in resolving problematic transactions. They employ professional mediators who negotiate solutions between sellers and buyers, resulting in satisfied customers—and even the removal of negative feedback. Additional information and monthly pricing structure is available at http://www.squaretrade.com.

Coordinate eBay with Your Own Web Site

Sellers with Web sites outside eBay can use the eBay's Merchant Kit (at http://pages.ebay.com/api/merchantkit.html) to help drive traffic from their Web site to their eBay sales. The kit provides easy-to-use HTML snippets to plug into the Web site code to insert all your current eBay listings automatically. The Merchant Kit includes customizing options to change the organization and appearance of the inserted eBay listing links. Of course, links resulting in the sale of goods from your eBay Store will qualify for the Store Referral Credit.

Use Third-Party Products for Complete E-Commerce Solutions

Many third-party developers offer fully customized e-commerce solutions that integrate easily with eBay sales. Services such as Kurant StoreSense, GoDaddy, ChannelAdvisor, and Marketworks assist businesses with Web development, marketing, inventory management, shopping cart, and checkout features.

Sellers maximize the advantages of selling via many channels by having an outside Web site. One advantage is to use the shopping cart feature of their off-eBay Web site as a checkout for eBay sales, allowing them to up-sell additional goods to their customers without incurring additional eBay fees. While these services come with heavy price tags, they are definitely the next level in e-commerce for the serious seller.

Note: eBay's summer 2005 introduction of ProStores aims to bring additional scalability to eBay businesses. With four levels of online storefronts, ProStores offers users advanced solutions for their e-commerce presence. These store levels include many customizable features, including shopping carts, real-time secure credit card processing, management of unlimited SKUs, integrated shipping (USPS, UPS, FedEx, and Canadian Post), a virtual inventory system, and advanced marketing and retention capabilities. Keep your eye on the eBay announcements boards so you'll know when the new program is rolled out.

Decisions, Decisions: The Best Tools for You

More and more private developers are building seamlessly integrated applications for eBay since eBay recently opened up its application and data structures to third parties. As a result, the number of programs available will skyrocket. Plus, the level of sophistication and specialization of these products will be out of this world.

That's both good and bad news. On the bright side, you'll see more and more applications that provide very specific value to your eBay selling methods. You'll be able to work faster, smarter, and more cost effectively by customizing a killer toolset for your own unique practices and business style. On the murkier side, you'll have to wade through a bunch of applications that may or may not do what you want. You'll have to rely on the eBay community and your business acumen to clear the confusion.

Think about it. You already have a lot of choices that must be made with the applications that exist. That's why you'll need to choose wisely (now and in the future). Ultimately your decisions about what to use will come down to some sort of cost and productivity analysis. You'll want to hit on some perennially important questions as you make evaluations, including these:

- How much time will the tool save you?
- Will it make you more money? And can you quantify that?
- Will you be able to reduce overhead (employees, services, space, sourcing costs, and so on)?

Fortunately, we've got some great resources that will help you decide. The following Web sites offer an incredibly comprehensive mix of product reviews, timely articles, detailed recommendations by industry and application, insider information, user forums, tools, and much more. Take it from us—these sites go deep. Spend some time at each and bookmark them all so you'll have a place to go when you need advice or direction:

- Auctionbytes.com
- AuctionSoftwareReview.com
- eCommerce-Guide.com

You also want to pay attention to eBay's Certified Provider Program. You can keep up with what's new by visiting http://developer.ebay.com/certifiedprovider from time to time. All the certified products are cataloged here, and multimedia presentations give you an in-depth look into how each of the software and services offerings work.

Be sure to visit the eBay Solutions Directory, too, at http://www
.solutions.ebay.com. This is the hub for all software and services solutions—
whether certified or not. You can search for specific solutions here, and
they're conveniently ranked by users. Once you click a particular product or
company, distinguish the bombs from the skyrockets by clicking the User
Rating column. This sorts them from best to worst.

Take some classes, read eBay books, drill into the help menus on the
site, and frequent the message boards. Use whatever learning method fits your
personality.

Recap

Use this chapter as a comprehensive resource or toolbox that you refer
back to and dip into frequently. We covered all kinds of tools for listing creation and management; sales and bid management; product configuration;
picture editing, managing, and hosting; fee calculation; shipping; traffic
generation; reporting; end-to-end e-commerce solutions; and more. We also
covered eBay Store basics and how to leverage this new format to your best
advantage.

Next, we're going to use these tools in the eBay context—with proven
marketing strategies—so you can get the most out of this book and pull the
most profit out of your auction and store sales. Let the fun begin!

Chapter 3

Putting a Face on Your eBay Brand: Critical Presentation and Visual Techniques

Poke around eBay and you'll find a wide array of item listings and eBay Stores whose visual statements range from the good and the bad to the downright ugly. You'll also find some really stellar examples of sellers who have integrated the appearance of their listings and their eBay Stores to create a cohesive online presence. Such efforts exude professionalism and inspire confidence in potential customers.

As we all know from our personal lives, critical judgments are made based on appearance. Imagine you're house hunting and your real estate agent shows up in sweatpants and a baseball cap. Would you trust this person's competence to handle this complex purchasing process? Conversely, if your child's baseball coach comes to practice still wearing his suit and tie from the office, you'd have serious doubts about his commitment to coaching the little league team.

The same holds true for your eBay business. Customers judge your dedication to your business by the appearance of your eBay Store and listings as well as the off-screen materials such as your business cards and packaging. You want every aspect of your business to present a consistent visual image that expresses your business personality and reinforces your brand. These efforts lend credibility and professionalism to your eBay business that pay off in increased sales and profits.

You can make the most of your presentation and business identity by following three basic strategies:

- Build your brand image by creating a visual or graphic identity.
- Use your brand image along with solid Web design principles in your item listings and eBay Store.
- Strengthen your brand image beyond the screen with printed materials and packaging that reflect your business identity.

Present a consistent look and feel throughout every aspect of your business. Doing so will make your business look more professional and reinforce your brand identity to customers.

Creating Your Own Graphic Identity

What exactly do we mean by a *graphic identity*? Most people think of business logos when they think of graphic identity. Designing a great logo is a major step in the process, but creating a graphic identity encompasses much more. It's about developing a complete system of graphical elements that represent your business. It's also about making conscientious decisions regarding all visual aspects of your business. It's determining a style, a look and feel for your business, and injecting that theme, with consistency, at any and every point at which you interface with customers. These decisions about your visual style help you create a harmonious visual message you can use in your eBay listings, eBay Store, printed materials, and beyond.

Your Business Personality and Your Image

So where do we begin? Think back to our branding discussion from Chapter 1, concerning your business personality and how that relates to your products and customer desires. These personality factors are major elements in the development of your eBay brand. Think about the visual associations that go along with your specialty or niche. If you sell women's beauty products, your visual style might reflect grace and femininity. If you sell scrapbooking materials, you might consider a style that is homespun or crafty. If you specialize in vintage art deco barware, a swanky retro look would be a great fit for your business. High-tech businesses obviously benefit from a streamlined, modern, or even futuristic appearance. Take a few moments with a pen and paper and brainstorm the sort of visual associations that fit your business.

Typefaces and Fonts Help Refine Your Look

The first step in creating a graphic identity for your business is easy: choose a typeface or font that suits your business personality. Typography is an incredible communication tool that conveys style and emotion well beyond the meaning of the words. The right font can work wonders in conveying your brand image. Once you've chosen an appropriate typeface, you can and should use your font of choice in everything from your logo and some aspects of your Web design to your invoices, stationery, and any other communication with your customers.

Experimenting with different typefaces is a great way to begin translating your business personality into a visual look. To identify fonts that work well for your business, try this exercise:

1. Open a blank Word document and type in your business name.
2. Copy and paste your business name 10 to 12 times.
3. For each copy of the name, select and apply different fonts from the pull-down font menu on the toolbar.

Note: Another web-savvy way to accomplish this is at http://www.dafont .com. This site offers hundreds of fonts along with a text box where you can type in your business name and preview it in any font they offer.

You should see how your choice of font can affect the perception of your business. You may see a particular font that accurately conveys your personality or brand. Figure 3-1 demonstrates how font choices convey different messages about several types of businesses.

The selection of fonts that come standard with MS Word, AppleWorks, or other commonly used document software is somewhat limited. If you're not finding a good fit from the standard list of fonts, you may want to shop around online for a more unique typeface. Dozens of Web sites offer samples and downloads of thousands of different fonts, many of which are freeware or shareware, and others can be purchased for a fee. A few free and small fee font sites include these:

- FontFreak (http://www.fontfreak.com)
- Acid Fonts (http://www.acidfonts.com)
- High Fonts (http://www.highfonts.com)
- Abstract Fonts (http://www.abstractfonts.com)

A quick Google search on the word *font* leads you to dozens of other font servers. Take the time to shop around and do some research until you find a font that communicates your business essence and sparks the desired emotional response in your customers.

Be sure to experiment with the font you choose. You'll use this font not just in creating your logo, but also in the printed correspondence you send to your customers. Type up and print out some sample documents to see if the font conveys the same feeling on paper as it does on your monitor. You also want to be sure that your text remains easy to read while still conveying the desired message about your brand. Creative, expressive fonts are really fun to use, but you need to be sure that your customers can decipher the content of your message; so whatever font you choose, make sure it's easily readable. Even if a font looks cool, if it's difficult to decipher, it will have an undesirable effect on your customers.

Sample Business Name	Font Name
ALI BABA RUGS	ALGERIAN
Collector's Books	Baskerville Old Face
Deco and Retro	Bauhaus 93
COMIX CORNER	Comic Sans MS
Fine Wines Online	Bradley Hand ITC
Scrapbook Supply	Gigi
Cowboy's Corral Western Gear	Playbill
THE COMPUTER DUDES	Impact
The Magician's Wand	Jokerman

Figure 3-1 This figure shows sample business names expressed with different fonts. Notice how the choice of font reflects the type of business and the perception of the brand.

> *Creative, expressive fonts are really fun to use, but you need to be sure that your customers can decipher the content of your message. Choose a font that represents your business personality but is still easy to read.*

You can use fonts for creating your logo and in printed customer correspondence (such as invoices, e-mails, and business cards). Take caution, however, when using an uncommon font for Web use—either in your eBay description, the text content of your eBay Store, or in e-mail. Unless the viewer's computer has the same font installed, the viewer won't see your text as you see it on your screen. This is why most Web sites (including eBay) limit their fonts to four of the most common typefaces: Times New Roman, Verdana, Arial, and Helvetica.

That's not to say that you should limit your font choice to one of these four ubiquitous fonts. (The printed world would be a visually boring place if that were the case!) Just bear in mind that if you use an uncommon font for your logo, you'll need to convert it to a graphics file (.jpg or .gif) for use on the Web. You can still use your signature font for printed materials, but you'll need to choose one of the four common fonts mentioned in the previous paragraph for the text of your eBay listings, e-mail text, or any other Web application. We'll discuss this idea in further detail as the chapter progresses.

Color and Your eBay Brand

Color can be a fun, easy, and effective way to build your eBay graphic identity. Large retailers and corporations use the power of color to convey brand messages. Think of Tiffany's robin's egg blue gift boxes and shopping bags, or the UPS brown logo, brown packaging, brown vans, and brown uniforms. Even the UPS slogan "What can Brown do for you?" incorporates the colorful brand message. Have you ever made the mistake of going shopping at Target wearing khaki pants and a red t-shirt? The other customers flog you with questions and requests for price checks because they've come to associate that color combination with Target and its employees.

Different colors are associated with distinct emotional connections. Use them to cultivate your eBay brand. Color associations include, but certainly aren't limited to, the following:

- **Green** Calming, environmentally friendly (Simple Green cleaning products)
- **Red** Intense, exciting (Red Envelope gifts, Red Hot Chili Peppers band)
- **Blue** Businesslike, contemplative (IBM "Big Blue," Miles Davis's album "Kind of Blue")
- **Purple** Mysterious, regal (musician Prince, the L.A. Lakers)
- **Pink** Femininity, innocence (Victoria's Secret, Johnson's Baby Lotion)
- **Yellow** Joyful, cheerful (Curious George books, rubber duckies)
- **Orange** Energetic, industrial (the Home Depot logo, men at work signs)

Ask yourself, "If my business were a color, what color would it be?" Yes, it does sound a little new agey, but by listing colors, you can make a color association that clicks with you and might make sense to your customers.

If you take the time to discover a color, or a scheme of complementary colors, that works for your business and its identity, you'll be able to incorporate this color into many aspects of your eBay business. It's a great way to add continuity to the design of your logo, the Web design of your eBay listings and store, printed items, packaging considerations, and more.

It's also important to remember not to go overboard with the use of color. Think of a bride planning her wedding and choosing her signature color. We've all been to weddings where the color theme is completely overdone: pink flowers, pink decorations, pink tablecloths and napkins, and those poor bridesmaids doused in pink from head to toe. However, if you choose the right color and use a little bit of restraint, adding it as design flourishes throughout your business, you'll create a theme that your customers can identify and appreciate. Color creates a visual-emotional cue that they'll come to associate with your business and your products. It strengthens your brand, inspires customers' confidence, and reinforces that emotional cue when they return as repeat customers.

Web-Safe Colors and Pantone Colors

The human eye perceives millions of different colors, in varying hues, shades, and saturation. To standardize this staggering array of color, both the printing and Web design worlds have developed systems for classifying color. When choosing a color to represent your business, it's a good idea to be familiar with these systems.

For Web design, 216 standard *web-safe* colors are available, with a corresponding HTML code to represent each color. These colors appear the same on any computer monitor, regardless of operating system, video card, or browser being used. An interactive chart showing these colors is available at http://www.visibone.com/colorlab.

For printing, Pantone (a registered trademark) is the recognized resource for the standardization of more than 3000 colors. Pantone has developed a matching system that guides professional printers in selecting, specifying, and matching ink colors. If you have an exact shade of brick red that you'd like to use for your logo, for example, your print shop will have a large palette of Pantone red colors, much like paint samples you find at a hardware store. You'll be able to choose that exact shade of red (or any other color you want), and it will be accurately represented in your printed materials.

Designing (or Redesigning) a Logo That Fits Your Business

A compelling logo that suits your business is a major brand strategy asset. A solid logo lends credibility and prestige to all other marketing efforts you put forth in your eBay business. You'll be able to use it on every eBay listing; in your eBay Store; on all of your invoices, business cards, e-mail communications, and packaging; and just about anywhere else your customer looks. A logo helps reinforce your brand message every time you interface with customers.

Why are logos so important? Psychologically speaking, images stick much better in people's minds than just words. A good logo makes an impact on customers, and it conveys the message of your brand. It sets your business apart from the crowd and makes it more memorable. It also gives your eBay business a more professional air, lending a sense of establishment and longevity. Customers are more likely to trust an eBay seller who has cultivated this sense of permanence with a solid logo, and they are more likely to remember eBay Stores with logo brands and return to shop on a repeat basis.

Your logo needs to be compatible with your brand image, and it should represent the personality of your business. It should be simple and visually easy for your customers to understand.

Note: A poorly designed and unprofessional looking logo is actually a detriment to your image. If you feel that you lack the creativity or skill to design your own logo, hiring a professional is a wise investment.

In this section, we'll help you focus the look of your logo. With a solid idea of what you'd like your logo to be, you can easily communicate your wishes to a designer. For the budget-conscious eBay seller, we'll show you some secrets to creating your own simple, yet professional-looking, logo.

Basic Considerations in Logo Design

We've all heard the old cliché, "I don't know much about art, but I know what I like." Well, the same holds true for most folks and logo designs. A great way to determine the style of your logo is to search and compile a reference file of other logos that you find appealing. You can find examples of existing logos that you see every day, from the food packaging in your pantry, to advertisements, letterhead, and packages you receive in the mail.

The Web offers another great resource. Google the word *logo,* and click the Images button on the menu bar to perform an image search. In less than a second, you see hundreds of logo images to peruse for inspiration.

Create a file of logos that appeal to you, either printing them out from online or clipping them from print sources as you come across them. You'll soon get a good idea of what you like and exactly what you want and don't want for your logo design. Use this file for your design inspiration, or share it with a professional designer to communicate the style of logo you want them to create.

If you've followed the suggestions from the earlier sections of this chapter and made some preliminary decisions about fonts and colors to convey your graphic identity, you're already on the path to a good logo design. Now consider any visual associations or images that you can link to your business identity. These associations could either come from the products you sell, from your business name, or from a generalized impression of your eBay brand.

Consider the adjectives used in describing your business "person." This helps guide the style and form these elements take in your logo design. Are you looking for a retro or classic look, a feeling of technology and the future, or something sleek or elegant? Brainstorm these associations and write them down. They'll be helpful as you proceed through this process.

The Three Basic Types of Logo Designs

When you look through your file of sample logos, you'll notice three basic types of logo design:

- The logotype design
- The illustrative logo design
- The symbolic logo design

The Logotype

The logotype design is a logo based on text only. Although seemingly easy to create, intense thought goes into even the simplest logotype designs. eBay, Dell Computers, and Yahoo! are a few examples of easily recognized logos in this style. Logotypes work best when the font selected embodies the brand. If you want to try this for yourself, revisit the existing font files on your computer, or go back to the font download Web sites, and take a second look at some of the creative fonts used. Reconsider some of the fonts that you found appealing but nixed because you couldn't see an entire business card printed in that typeface. Could your logo be your business name forged in one of these expressive fonts in your signature color? If you decide to go this route, be sure to choose an easy-to-read complementary font for other text that appears in your correspondence. For the sake of your customers' vision and sanity, use this complementary font for all text other than your business name in the logotype.

The Illustrative Logo

The illustrative logo uses a figural or representative image as part of the logo design, usually in combination with the business name. For example, an eBay bookseller may naturally gravitate toward an image of an open book as part of an illustrative logo. Some examples of well-known illustrative logos are Apple Computer, the National Basketball Association (NBA), and Starbucks. If you are artistically inclined, go ahead and create your own logo illustration.

Copyright-free clip art is another possibility for logo images, but it should be chosen with extreme care. Most available clip art positively screams "I am clip art!" and using it for your logo can seem trite and cheesy, unless you choose an absolutely perfect match for your business. Again, some things are best left to the pros, so if you truly lack artistic skill, hire a graphic designer.

Symbolic Logos

Symbolic logos employ abstract designs or images that connote a basic feeling about a business. Swooshes and circles are popular in logo design for their feeling of movement. The Nike Swoosh logo is the classic example. Stylized initials and letters also make great abstract symbols to use as a logo. Walk into any parking lot and you'll find dozens of symbolic logos as hood ornaments—Mercedes-Benz, Toyota, Saturn, BMW. We all know them by sight, without having to read the manufacturer's name.

Figure 3-2 shows a variety of logos in different formats that are currently in use on eBay.

Consider these basic formats and the elements you wish to include in your logo design. Start with a pen and paper and sketch out as many possibilities and variations as you can imagine. Sleep on it, and then sketch some more. Share your logo musings with your friends for feedback—second and third opinions offer a lot of insight. From here, you'll be able to build your own logo or pass on your sketches to a professional designer so she can turn it into something wonderful.

Further Considerations to Your Logo Design

Once you've established the elements you want to include in your logo and mapped out your basic design, you should make a few additional design considerations.

If you're going to create a logo yourself, you'll need to have access to image-editing software such as Adobe Illustrator or PhotoShop. Even if you use a creative font for a logotype design, you'll still need to use such software to convert this into either a .jpg or .gif image file for use on the Web, and .tif or .eps for print applications.

Consider your logo's size and scalability. You'll need to make the image smaller or larger for use in different formats. Crisp, uncomplicated lines work best. Keep illustrative designs simple so details don't get lost when you scale it down to business card size. Also consider your file resolution. You want to have a higher resolution file for clarity when printing and lower resolution (72 dpi) for quick downloads on the Web.

Figure 3-2 Shown here are logos used by eBay sellers. Represented are logotype, illustrative, and symbolic logos.

Caution: For Web applications, your logo should have a low resolution (72 dpi). Otherwise, it could take a long time for customers to download the image, and they could get sidetracked and go to another seller's site.

Think about your use of color and how it affects your printing costs. One- and two-color designs can be printed for a fairly reasonable cost, but add colors and your printing costs increase exponentially. Single-color logos make strong graphic statements and work well for businesses under tight budgets.

Finally, consider the proportions of your logo. On the eBay Store page is a field in which a seller can insert a link to his own logo at the top of the page. This field is a rectangular format with a 3.5 to 1 ratio. If you try to plug a square or circular logo into this field, it will become skewed and distorted. You may wish either to create your logo in these proportions from the start or create a secondary and complementary design in a rectangular format to enter into this space.

Tip: The eBay Store logo field is a key piece of real estate for developing your brand. eBay also uses the contents of this field as thumbnails for displaying Anchor Stores subscriptions in the eBay Stores directory. Be sure to use this golden opportunity to insert your eBay brand.

Once you've made some decisions about your overall graphic identity and created a logo that strongly represents your business, you're ready to put that design sense to work in your eBay listings and eBay Store.

Do-It-Yourself Logo Design Online

Just when you think the Internet couldn't possibly make your life any easier, along comes a service like LogoYes (http://www.logoyes.com/ebay) and proves that it can. This Web site has a fun and user-friendly interface that helps you design your own logo. With its "try before you buy" feature, users are guided through six easy steps to building their own logo.

The program allows you to choose the style of your illustrative element, be it "high-tech" for the innovative or technically advanced, "bold" for the experienced and trustworthy, or "flair" for creative and customer-responsive businesses. Choose from a wide variety of images categorized by industry type. Lay out your image with your business name, tagline, or any other text. Choose from among 24 fonts and a rainbow of colors. It's easy to edit, change, scale, flip, or rotate any or all elements until you've created a logo that pleases you.

Once you have a design you like, you can purchase it for $99, which entitles you to .jpg and .gif files to use on the Web, .eps files for printing, and 250 free business cards. You even have the option of creating two different logos and e-mailing them to your friends so they can offer feedback or vote on which one they like. It's an easy and fun way to make an expressive and professional-looking logo.

LogoYes offers special packages for eBay sellers. Along with the standard logo format, they'll include a secondary logo formatted specifically to the 3.5 to 1 ratio for eBay Stores. Go to http://www.logoyes.com/ebay for samples of eBay logos created with LogoYes.

Designing Your eBay Listings and eBay Store

In Chapter 2, we introduced tools such as the eBay Store and Turbo Lister with Listing Designer, as well as services from third-party providers that help you create a cohesive online selling presence. These tools offer you powerful Web-design capabilities and are so user-friendly that anyone can build a professional-looking eBay Store and listings. This is a perfect opportunity to use your graphic identity and customize your eBay selling presence. With these tools, you can create a consistent design and recurring theme throughout your listings and eBay Store. The combined effect reinforces your brand and identity.

Paying attention to these design opportunities makes your products more appealing. It makes it easier for your customers to view and appreciate your products. Your eBay Store is easier to navigate, and your items are easier to find. Your customers receive a very distinct message about your eBay brand that encourages them to buy and return to buy some more. Ultimately, you enjoy more sales and more profit.

Hire a Pro, or Do It Yourself

Many sellers are so devoted to cultivating their online presence that they employ professionals to develop truly customized eBay Storefront interfaces and listing templates. Several of the third-party listing management services discussed in Chapter 2 offer customized Web design services as part of their packages. (See the eBay Certified Provider page at http://developer.ebay.com/certifiedprovider for more detailed information.) One recommended site is http://www.elance.com. This site allows you to place a free request for a variety of professional services and professional designers will bid on the project. In addition, many Web designers create custom design packages for eBay sellers. You can find a list of links to designers-for-hire under the Web Design & Development category on the eBay Professional Services Page located at http://pages.ebay.com/business_services.

In Chapter 1, we showed an example of eBay Store design of the 2004 Best of Stores winner, Frenchy Bee. This is the perfect example of an eBay seller who has developed an eBay Store with an integrated listing template design that truly captures the brand essence of the business. The winning store design was created by eBay design gurus, The Pix Clinic. They understand the importance of building an eBay brand and have developed a "personality package"—a combination of design services that help eBay sellers build their brand. For more information, visit http://www.pixclinic.com.

Naturally, custom Web-design services come at a price. However, there's no need to fret if professional design services aren't within your reach. The HTML editing and template tools offered by eBay and other third-party services are so flexible and powerful that anyone can create a professional-looking online selling presence. These tools come at very reasonable prices, and some are even free, so you can do it yourself at a fraction of the cost of professional Web designers' fees. Whether you choose to have a designer create custom templates or you do it yourself with existing templates on eBay, you can maximize the visual impact of your eBay presence. We'll show you how.

What Is Web Usability?

Web usability is a fairly new catch phrase in the design world that refers to measuring the quality of a visitor's experience on a particular Web site, including your eBay listings and Store. Usability addresses questions about how easily the visitor can find the information she is seeking and how pleasant her experience is on the site. It is the study of Web aesthetics, navigation, and accessibility of information.

We've all suffered through Web sites with poor usability. They are riddled with pop-ups, advertisements, difficult to read text, obnoxious graphics, illogical organization, and worse. The result of this poor usability is wasted time and intense frustration. We quickly click away to another site, never to return.

As the Web continues to grow, its users are becoming more sophisticated by the moment. Most users have an extremely low tolerance for poor design. Your customers know good Web design when they see it, and it's important that you give it to them. Good usability design lends your business the mark of professionalism and distinguishes you from competitors.

Designing Your Online Presence in Your eBay Listings

We've established the importance of continuity with your graphic identity—your eBay brand is strengthened if you create your online presence with the same sort of consistency. In this section, we discuss what constitutes good Web design and uncover many tips and tricks of professional Web designers that you can use in your own listings and eBay Store.

As you read through this section, consider the ways that you can create an ongoing visual theme that represents your brand identity. We'll begin this discussion on creating a visual message in your eBay listings, but the same visual theme ties into the design of your eBay Store. The colors, typeface, backgrounds, borders, and overall style you choose should be the same in all of your listings and eBay Store. We'll also discuss ways to insert your logo at every opportune moment to drive home a solid branding message to your online visitors.

Content Is King

The Number 1 rule of good Web design is "content is king." This holds particularly true for your eBay listings. The first priority of your listing design is to showcase your goods for sale in the most flattering light possible and within the context of your broader business image. The last thing you want to do is distract the viewer's attention from the item he is considering purchasing.

eBay's Turbo Lister, Listing Designer, and other third-party listing services such as Vendio, InkFrog and Mpire all offer WYSIWYG (What You See Is What You Get) HTML editors. The primary mistake that many sellers make when they get their hands on a WYSIWYG editor is that they go way overboard with bells and whistles. They use busy backgrounds and too many different fonts, colors, and type sizes (or even worse, animations, music, and scrolling banners). By the time the listing is created, it looks like a kaleidoscope. The listing viewer becomes confused and distracted, not to mention turned off by an unprofessional-looking site.

Tip: Reduce the amount of bells and whistles on your eBay listings and Store designs. Since over half of the country is still using dial-up, putting extraneous items in your listings creates slower downloads and may drive your customers to your competitors.

Such "design" efforts are counterproductive to the selling of merchandise. The old adage "less is more" could not be more true in this case. Thoughtful design decisions, mitigated with a bit of restraint, tone down all the visual "noise." The point is for your design to complement, rather than compete with, the item that you wish to sell.

Remember that content is king. Less is more. The point of your listing design is to complement, rather than compete with, the item that you wish to sell.

Selecting Colors, Backgrounds, and Borders

Returning to our discussion of using color to build your brand, the color scheme you choose for your eBay listings (and consequentially, your eBay Store) plays a major part in developing a strong online presence. If you use eBay's Listing Designer or the templates offered from third-party listing services, you'll find that they all come with a variety of options for choosing background colors and border designs. They make it easy to incorporate your design theme and color scheme into every listing. Think of your signature color and the logo you've designed when browsing the options available in these listing services, and choose a style that complements your brand image.

Once again, considering that your content is king, make a template background selection that won't compete with the items you're selling. As you browse the designs available, note that many template designs use borders with cute or clever designs of baby blocks, flowers, and other themed images. While it may be tempting to use these designs, make sure that your customers' attention remains focused on the item you're selling. You don't want to distract them with a busy border or patterned background. If you choose a fairly neutral template with a solid background and simple borders, you'll be able to use it for *all* your listings, adding to the desired consistency of design that builds brand identity.

Keeping It All "Above the Fold"

"Above the fold" is an old newspaper journalism term that has been reappropriated in the Web design world. Think of the way that the most important headlines and photos are laid out on the newspaper front page to fit above the horizontal crease. This allows the viewer to see as much essential information and images as possible in a single view. In Web design, *above the fold* refers to the amount of the Web page the user views on the screen without having to scroll down. For eBay listings, keeping important information above the fold is particularly important. You want your potential customers to get as much information as possible within a single view of the screen.

When you go into any eBay item listing page, the view you'll immediately see above the fold is eBay's own information with the title, item number, seller information, and bidding information.

Figure 3-3 depicts the standard view of the screen that appears when users open any eBay listing page. Unfortunately, the part of the listing that you have power to control (the description and more images) never appears above the fold. However, you should design your listing layout so that once the viewer has scrolled once, she will be able to view your item description and its images in one screen without having to scroll much more.

Just as newspaper readers are less likely to continue reading a story that goes below the fold, the same holds true for scrolling and eBay customers. Remember that it's as easy for a potential customer to click off your site as it is for him to scroll all over your page. You want to keep his attention on your item until he has become engaged in what you're selling. You need to do everything in your power to keep his hand off that mouse until he's ready to click the bid button.

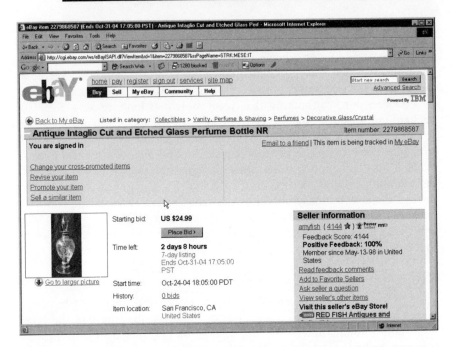

Figure 3-3   Above the fold view of typical eBay listing. Note that this is standard eBay information; the viewer must scroll down to see the seller's item description and images.

Using Tables in Your Listing Layout

One of the inherent flaws in using the standard eBay sell form is that the layout places the text first and images at the bottom. Buyers find it irritating to have to scroll down to the bottom to see pictures of the item. And when they have to do so, the seller also runs the risk of the dreaded "click factor." Using HTML to embed photos into the item description partially solves this problem but tends to increase the necessity for the user to scroll down even more.

The best solution to this problem is to utilize tables in your item listing. An HTML table allows you to lay out your item listing with images and text side by side. eBay's Listing Designer and other third-party listing design tools all offer the table option. Table usage is Web-standard practice. If you hire someone to custom design a template, you should be sure that she includes HTML tables in your listing templates.

Tables increase the usability of your listing. With this effective layout technique, potential customers can see the images and read the description at the same time, with minimal scrolling and clicking. It's the combination of the visual cue of the image with the information of text that keeps the viewer engaged with your listing. This prevents boredom and click-aways and inspires purchases. Figure 3-4 demonstrates an HTML table format layout in an eBay listing.

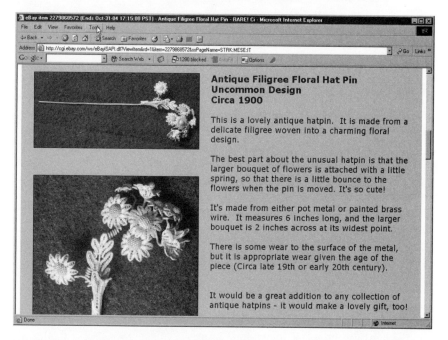

Figure 3-4 Sample eBay listing using HTML table layout with images to the left and text to the right. Note how the seller keeps the pertinent information above the fold.

Creating a Hierarchy of Information

Naturally, some eBay listings end up being longer than a single scroll of the screen. This is where it becomes important to determine a hierarchy of your information—in other words, present the most important information first, followed by extra details, and then your conditions of sale. We will elaborate on the importance of creating a hierarchy of ideas in Chapter 4. But for now, bear in mind the importance of creating a hierarchy of information so that the most persuasive text and images stay above the fold.

Choosing Photo View Options

eBay and third-party listing design services offer options for photo presentation. The standard, static view is a 400×300 pixel image, but options are available to "supersize" photos, zoom stream for close-ups, and select multi-image photo album style views and 360-degree views that allow customers to toggle around all sides of an object.

So which is best to use? Two schools of thought exist when it comes to making this image display decision. Proponents of using static images argue that if you supply several views of an item and use an HTML table to lay out the images alongside the text, customers are presented with a clear and concise message about the product. They also believe that these alternative means of image display are gimmicks that simply distract the customers from the item for sale.

Proponents of the special views claim that using zoom, 360-degree, and supersize features make their listings more dynamic and better engage the viewer in the item for sale. They argue that giving the customer an active role in viewing the images is an empowering experience and makes her more likely to buy.

Both camps have legitimate points, so this is ultimately a decision that every eBay seller must make for himself or herself. The option you choose may even vary from one item to the next, depending on the nature of what you're selling. The most important thing is that you use clear images that illustrate your product effectively, no matter which way you choose to display them online.

Tips on Effective Digital Photography

Volumes have been written on effective digital photography techniques for eBay listings. For the purposes of brevity, we're including a few of the most essential tips for winning images:

- Create a photo staging area with a solid-colored background and foreground. A wrinkle-free, solid color bed sheet spread between two chairs works great.
- Use good lighting. Natural light works well, or use two clip lights (covered with tracing paper to reduce reflections) and angle them on either side of your object for a shadow-free image.
- Get in close to your object so that it fills most of the camera's frame. Too much blank space around your object makes it appear small.
- Take images of different angles and views of your object, and take several shots from each angle so you'll have a variety of pictures from which to choose. It's much easier to delete extra image files than to have to go back and photograph again.
- Use the macro lens on your camera to capture small details and use a tripod or a very steady hand to keep a tight focus.
- Use image-editing software to crop, rotate, and resize your images. (We mentioned several inexpensive image-editing software options in Chapter 2.)

- Reduce image sizes to under 50K for quick downloads. Your image width should be no more than 500 pixels, and 72 dpi is optimum resolution for Web viewing. Higher resolutions do not yield better images on screen, and lower resolutions become too pixilated. (Most digital cameras automatically shoot in 72 dpi, but if you use a scanner for flat objects, be sure to change your dpi capture setting.)

- Buyers prefer multiple views of an item. Give them shots from all sides, as well as close-ups and detail photos. As discussed in Chapter 2, invest in a flat-rate image hosting service so you'll feel free to post multiple images for each listing without worrying about extra fees.

- Use your photos to reinforce your brand and graphic identity. Keep a consistent look of lighting, staging, composition, and background for the images of everything you sell. Choose a background for your photos that will complement the HTML background you've chosen for your item listing.

If you feel that your digital photography skills need further improvement, consult one of the many "nuts-and-bolts" type eBay instruction books on the market that offer elaborate photography tips. Dennis Prince's *How to Sell Anything on eBay . . . and Make a Fortune!* (McGraw-Hill, 2003) has a great chapter on the nuances of digital photography.

Design Your Item Description Text for Better Usability

A few easy tricks make your item listing text easier to read and more visually appealing to your customers. First, use headlines and subheads to highlight important features and break up sections of your text. Create an item headline in larger, boldface type at the top of every item description. A headline is great for repeating the information in the item's title, without the usual abbreviations and 55-character limitation. The headline reminds the viewer exactly what they're looking at, and helps keep all of the item's pertinent information within a single screen view. If you look back again at the screenshot in Figure 3-4, you'll notice that the seller utilized this headlining technique.

You can also use subheads to highlight additional information. They can appear under a headline at the top of the page to draw the viewer's attention to other key features of the item for sale. You can also create subheads to designate different sections of your item description, such as "Conditions of Sale" or "Shipping Information." Chapter 4 discusses headlines and subheads as a means of marketing your product with effective copywriting.

"Chunking" Text and Negative Space

Another way to create visual appeal and increase usability (and readability) is to divide your item description into chunks of text. Onscreen reading is different from reading printed text, and it's easy for viewers to lose their place or become confused by endless streams of words. Divide your text into short paragraphs that convey either a single idea or a few simple ideas. Then use your HTML editor to put an extra line of blank space between each paragraph to give it a chunky effect.

> **Tip:** Aligning your text to the left is Web-standard design for better usability. You'll also notice that the first words of paragraphs are seldom indented online. In addition, centered and right-aligned text should be used with caution, as it can be difficult for the reader to negotiate.

Chunking your text creates *negative space,* or *white space,* an important aspect of good design. Negative space—small, blank areas between images, graphic elements, and text—creates visual organization and guides the viewers' eyes from one element to the next. When you use the listing templates provided by eBay's Listing Designer, the HTML tables are automatically laid out so that negative space appears between the photos you add and the area where you enter the item description. All you'll need to do is continue using negative space in your description text to complete the picture. If you hire a designer to create your own custom listing templates, be sure she considers the use of negative space in her design.

> **Caution:** It is possible to include too much negative space. You don't want to make your viewer scroll too much. Or worse, the viewer may think that nothing else resides below the screen and therefore won't bother to scroll down at all. Use just enough negative space to rest the viewer's eye. Keep it in proportion and try to keep important information above the fold.

Font Style, Size, and Color

A few final considerations are worth noting when designing the text in your item description. First, don't forget about the complications of your font selection for Web use. As mentioned earlier, if you use an unusual font, your viewer's computer needs to be installed with the same font if she is going to see the font as you do on your own screen.

As also mentioned, stick with Web-safe fonts such as Times New Roman, Verdana, Arial, and Helvetica to ensure that the text reads the same on any user's computer. Which should you choose? Times New Roman and Verdana have a classic and sophisticated appearance. Arial and Helvetica have a more modern and contemporary look. If you use a logotype font, remember to convert your logo to a .gif or .jpg file for use on your eBay listings and store.

The size of your text is also important. Too small is tough to read, and too large means your customer has to scroll around unnecessarily. A 12-point font size is appropriate for the body text or your paragraphs, and 14 to 18 points is a good size for headers or subheads. Reserve boldface, italics, and all capital letters for use in headings or subheads. If you have to, use them sparingly in body text. Entire paragraphs rendered in italic or all caps are very difficult to read.

You'll also want to choose a text color that creates a strong contrast with your background color. It's best to use a standard dark color on a light background. You may be tempted to try the design trick of reverse type, where light colors are used on dark backgrounds, but we don't suggest you do this. Even with a strong contrast of type versus background, reverse type is distinctly more difficult to read and can cause viewers to click away from your listing.

Finally, the color selection of your type should remain consistent throughout all your listings and your eBay Store. Using too many colors creates visual noise. Decide on a single color that complements your overall graphic identity and stick with it to make your listings more pleasant to view and your brand message clearer.

Use Your Logo in Your Listings

The final step to forging your brand presence in your eBay listings is to insert your logo into each listing you create. If you have a professional designer create custom templates for you, your logo can be incorporated into the overall design. However, if you use the existing templates from Listing Designer or other similar services, you can still insert your logo into the text with simple HTML code. You can even turn your logo into a hot spot that, when clicked, links the customer to your eBay Store. Here's how:

1. Upload your .jpg or .gif image file of your logo to your image-hosting service.
2. In the Enter Your Description section of the listing, choose the View HTML option.
3. Scroll down through the code to the spot where you wish to insert your logo and enter these two HTML tags:

```
<A href="http://(type your eBay Store URL)">
<img src="http://(type the URL for your logo image)">
```

Tip: You can take these HTML tags and create a macro to make it easy to insert your logo into every listing. On eBay's Sell Your Item form, as well as on Turbo Lister, the function is available under the Insert pull-down menu on the toolbar.

With your logo as a hot spot, you'll create a very important navigational link to your eBay Store. Inserting links in your eBay listings that connect customers to your eBay Store is the smartest and easiest way to drive traffic to your store. You can generate even more sales. (Chapter 5 discusses how to insert these links in your listings as a means of cross-selling and up-selling your products to your customers.) The next section discusses ways to design your eBay Store so that it's consistent with your listings and further strengthens your brand.

Design Considerations for Your eBay Store

Your eBay Store consolidates your brand presence on eBay. As the nexus of all your eBay selling activity, your eBay Store should be designed to coordinate with your listings. The eBay Store is the perfect place to layer on another brand message. Creating a polished store design gives your business a professional appearance that inspires trust in your customers and encourages their buying behavior (and that last step, encouraging buying behavior, is the whole point of building your brand).

Whether you use professional custom design services or do it yourself, the basic structure of the eBay Store presents many opportunities to build your eBay brand. In Chapter 2, we took you step-by-step through the process of creating your store. Refer back to Chapter 2 if you find you need a refresher course as you read through this next section. We'll focus on how you can use that basic setup to create an online presence that impresses your individual brand on prospective customers. All of these options are available by clicking the Manage Your Store link at the bottom of your store home page.

Customize Your Store Appearance to Build Your Brand

You can customize your eBay Store's appearance in several ways to send strong brand messages to your customers:

- *Choose your store theme.* Choose your overall store design to complement your brand's color theme and style. Use the preset store design templates or customized store design wizard, or create an HTML design on your own or with the help of a designer.
- *Extend your store theme.* Use the same design theme for all custom pages you create. You also want to match the theme to the HTML template design used for your individual item listings.

- *Use your logo.* With your Store Design page, insert your custom logo into your store's customized header so that it appears at the top of every page in your eBay Store. Remember that this is prime real estate for forging your brand identity, so don't miss this opportunity.
- *Don't forget the custom listing header.* Create a custom listing header to appear automatically at the top of each item listing. Use the same color scheme and design, and insert your custom logo and links to take customers to your eBay Store.

Tip: Remember that design consistency gives strength to your brand message, so choose a visual theme and insert it at every point where your customers view your goods on eBay.

Make Your eBay Store Easy to Navigate

Along with an aesthetically pleasing graphic identity, successful eBay Store designs require ease of navigation. Even if you've designed the coolest or most beautiful eBay Storefront, you won't make many sales if your customers have a hard time finding what they're looking for. An eBay Store with good Web usability presents the items for sale in a concise and logical manner. This allows viewers to understand intuitively how to navigate through the store and find what they seek.

You can customize your store for easy usability in several ways. Remember that creation and editing functions are accessed through your Manage Your Store page.

- *Maximize your custom categories.* Use the 19 customizable store categories to your best advantage. Categorize your items by the type of product or brand name, or even by size (particularly helpful for clothing or shoes). Or use categories to highlight sale items or new arrivals. Categories are the virtual aisles of your eBay Store, so think about logical associations between items and group them appropriately.
- *Customize the appearance of your listing icons.* Choose to display your listings with a Gallery image view or display them in a text-only list. A list view is perfect if you have long lists of items in which the image is not as important as the descriptions. For items that rely on pictures or photos to generate appeal, use the Gallery view option to spark customer interest.
- *Set different defaults for the displayed view of your items.* Choose from Ending Soonest (to display items that tend to garner lots of last-minute sniper bidding) or by Lowest Price (for bargain-oriented businesses to display their goods).

- *Create custom pages for easy browsing.* Much like a standard Web site design, eBay custom pages can be created to provide quick links to different information. Use custom pages as your store home page or landing page, to showcase new inventory, highlight items on sale, disclose your store policies or shipping information, give a history or overview of your business, or display just about any other information you'd like to share with your customers.

Note: Your eBay Store design and usability is an integral part of your complete brand message. Good design shows that you care for your customers and strive to make their shopping experience as delightful as possible.

Beyond the Screen: Using Your Brand in Printed Materials and Packaging

Once the deal is done and you're ready to send the goods to the buyer, you have a final opportunity to convey a strong brand message to your customer with the printed materials and packaging you use for shipping. This is a step that many eBay sellers don't bother with. However, missing this final chance is a big mistake. Every package you send is a unique direct advertising opportunity and has the potential to turn a one-time buyer into a loyal customer.

Custom stationery and attention to packaging conveys professionalism and steadfastness. It also makes your brand more memorable to your customers and draws them back to your eBay Store to shop some more. Chapter 6 delves deeper into strategies that build customer satisfaction and retention. Great-looking printed business cards and stationery will be a crucial part of this strategy, and this section shows you how to create them.

Printed Graphic Identity Materials

Once you have designed your logo, it's easy to create a printed graphic identity package. Create simple layouts of your logo using your contact information for letterhead and business cards. This gives your business some clout, as if you've been around for years, even if you're still a little green. Use existing templates in Microsoft Word or other software to design your own layouts, or employ a professional printer to lay out your stationery for you.

Experiment with the placement of your logo and your contact information on letter-sized paper, as well as with business card formats. And remember that simplicity is best: Don't try to cram too much information on your business card; stick to the essential contact information. Remember that your signature font can help drive your brand, too, so use it in your printed materials. Be sure to include your eBay Store URL on all your printed materials to drive business back to the store.

Tip: eBay offers customizable business card and stationery templates that are free to use for eBay Stores subscribers. To view and download the templates, go to http://pages.ebay.com/storefronts/collateral.html.

While it's tempting for budget-conscious businesses to print letterhead and business cards on a home printer, it's worth investigating professional printing options. Professional printing is not as pricey as you might think, and if you intend to create even a small volume of printed materials, it's actually more cost effective than purchasing expensive products like the perforated business card stock that you print yourself. Your final product ends up being much higher quality and sends buyers a strong message of your commitment to your business.

Tip: You can get free, professionally printed business cards, as well as discount printing on letterhead, envelopes, brochures, self-adhesive stickers, and much more, through VistaPrint, an online printing service (http://www .vistaprint.com). VistaPrint has preformed templates and custom design options for a variety of marketing and branding printed materials.

The two must-have printed pieces are *letterhead* and *business cards*. Use your letterhead for printing professional-looking invoices and additional promotional materials. Place business cards in every package you ship, and use them to promote your business in person-to-person situations. Be sure to choose quality paper and coordinating business cardstock. Carefully select the paper and ink colors to reflect your brand image. Be cautious of patterned or textured papers as they can detract from your logo or your contact information. Remember that your stationery has two purposes:

- To disperse your contact information to customers
- To further the consistency and strength of your eBay brand image

Handle with Care: Packaging Considerations

Traditional retailers understand the importance of packaging in consumer perceptions of their products. Packaging makes or breaks the customer's impression of a product, and interesting packaging really makes an item fly off the shelves. In e-commerce situations, the importance of packaging shifts from the product itself to the materials used to ship the goods directly to the customer. Quality shipping materials increase the customer's perceived value of a product when it is delivered to them.

Quality shipping materials increase the customer's perceived value of a product when it is delivered to them.

It's amazing how many eBay sellers get this angle all wrong. The temptation to save money by skimping on shipping materials is great, but if it decreases the chances of a customer returning to your eBay Store to purchase more, then you're actually losing money, not saving it.

Imagine you're a customer who just purchased an expensive crystal vase, and it's shipped to you wrapped in shabby, reused bubble wrap and nestled in a recycled Pampers box. Suddenly, your excitement about the vase is diminished, and it just doesn't seem as special or valuable as when you viewed it online. And you likely won't be returning to that seller's eBay Store to purchase anything else.

> **Tip:** Shipping materials are expensive, so it's important to build that cost into the price of your item or your handling charges, and then deliver the goods with packaging that reflects the quality and value of the product inside.

Printed shipping labels ooze with professionalism. Compare your reaction to receiving a package with a crisp printed label as opposed to a package with the address sloppily scrawled in magic marker. One promises to contain an earthly delight, and the other looks like it may have come from the Unabomber. To address your packages professionally (with the option to print your own postage), use the self-printed shipping labels offered through eBay via USPS (US Postal Service) or UPS. You can also create an account with Pitney Bowes, UPS, FedEx, or other shippers directly for printed label and postage options. Or try a third-party postage server such as Endicia.com or Stamps.com.

> **Tip:** Along with Endicia's postage printing service, the company also offers a fabulous mail design tool that allows sellers to design their own envelopes, mailings, and shipping labels. You can use your own logo and other graphics to design your own shipping label that reflects your brand identity. You can customize multiple designs and use them to print USPS postage, too. For more information, go to http://www.endicia.com/endicia-usa/Site/design.cfm.

Lastly, use your shipping materials as an opportunity to strengthen your eBay brand. Sellers with a large volume of products find it worth having boxes custom printed with their business name and logo. If you ship smaller amounts of goods, consider printing your logo on self-adhesive labels that can be used to customize any box or packaging. Use your brand's color scheme in your shipping materials, too. Bubble wrap and tissue paper come in a wonderful variety of colors that can add that final hint of your brand when your customer opens the box. It's an inexpensive way to reaffirm your brand.

Tip: Chiswick Packaging Solutions (http://www.chiswick.com) is a great resource for personalized, branded packaging materials. The company custom prints corrugated boxes, packaging tape, self-adhesive stickers, and padded mailers. You can also purchase bulk shipping materials, colored tissue, and much more.

Details, Details, Details

Don't sweat the small stuff? Nothing could be less true when you're creating your eBay brand identity. All of the suggestions in this chapter may seem like insignificant steps individually, but when you put them all together, they create a consistent brand message to which customers really respond.

Considering all of these nit-picky details, it's a good idea to create written guidelines on the use of your graphic identity. If you have employees, written guidelines can help with consistency, and if you work alone, it helps you avoid cutting corners when you get busy. Your written guidelines should cover decisions about the ideas we've discussed in this chapter, including the following:

- Your choice of font, color, and other graphic identity decisions
- When and where to use your logo
- Standardization of design for item listings
- Stationery layout and choice of card stock for printing
- Directives for stationery use with invoices, customer letters, and other communication

Making written guidelines about your graphic identity and design issues creates a standard of quality that pervades your business and strengthens your brand. And strong brand identity gives you an edge for success.

Recap

Now that we've covered graphic identity, let's move on to Chapter 4, where we share professional copywriters' secrets for writing persuasive item descriptions. But before we do, here's a recap of some important topics of this chapter:

- Create a graphic identity for your business. Determine a style, look, and feel. Interject that theme, with consistency, at any and every point where you interface with customers.
- Create a "look" that represents the personality of your business. Choose your signature font and color with care.

- Design a logo that suits your business and reinforces your brand.
- Create an effective Web design theme from your listings and eBay Store. Use that theme with consistency to strengthen your brand.
- Remember the goal of good Web usability. Your content is king, and less is more. Don't go nuts with your WYSIWYG HTML editor.
- Try to keep important information above the fold in your item listings. Use HTML tables to lay out images beside text. Create a hierarchy of information so the most important and attention-grabbing information is toward the top.
- Chunk your text and use headlines and subheads to make your text easy to read. Carefully select your font size and color for better readability, too.
- Make the most of your photos. Use every trick up your photography sleeve to present the best images possible for your merchandise.
- Make your eBay Store design cohesive with the visual look of your listings. Customize your store so it's logical and easy to navigate.
- Create printed materials such as letterhead, business cards, and packaging that reflect your graphic identity and help build your brand. Use them at every possible opportunity.

Chapter 4

Sell Anyone Anything with Words:
Effective Copywriting Techniques

A picture *is* worth 1000 words. However, the words are summoned by the viewer, not the seller. You could show two people a picture of a puppy, and one would say "adorable," the other "fleabag." The picture is open to thousands of interpretations.

For that reason, when you write your eBay descriptions, you want to complement your visual achievements (photos and layout/design) with words that manage perceptions while presenting facts. You want to stoke the flames of enthusiasm while staying true to reality.

Nobody buys anything without being told something about it—whether that's in verbal or written form. So it's important to choose your words wisely and engage in the art and science of persuasion in each of your eBay listings. When you take the time to craft a strong item description, you inevitably persuade people to buy from you. It doesn't matter whether you have competition or not—you need to convince somebody to purchase what you're selling. Solid item descriptions help you do that.

In this chapter, we cover writing fundamentals (and some added tips and tricks) that transform repellant, snooze-fest descriptions into magnets of commerce. We show you how to do the following:

- Organize your work
- Align your thoughts with the customer experience
- Format your writing for optimal appeal
- Write like a pro
- Assemble the optimal mix of keywords
- Create eye-catching headlines
- Fine-tune your descriptions

We also unveil some trade secrets from professional advertising copywriters that help you write descriptions quickly, easily, and profitably.

Organize Your Listings

The first step is organizing: For each item you sell, you want to make an analysis of your effort versus your profit. Obviously, if you stand to make $500 in profit on a particular item, it's worth your time to craft an effective description. But even if you're selling a large quantity of low-margin items with just one listing, the extra time it takes to write a good item description is worth the trouble. If you are selling 100 gadgets and you can potentially profit by $5 on each of them, that's a total of $500 in your pocket. It's definitely worth taking an extra 30 minutes to write a powerful item description.

When you start prioritizing your description tasks, put items into mental buckets. Use one bucket for products that need your attention now. Make another bucket for low-margin items you might want to re-evaluate for value-added activities (perhaps overhauling the description text), and then use another bucket for products that can be dealt with quickly by cutting and pasting previously successful descriptions. Think assembly line here; you need a system that guides your priorities and steers you toward high-value or high-profit marketing activities.

Fortunately, eBay automates the cut-and-paste process as a free service. The Sell Similar link at the top of every item listing page (and in the My eBay interface) lets you pull up previously entered listing details, which you can revise and apply to a new listing. Sellers who use listing management services like eBay's Turbo Lister or similar third-party services can also duplicate existing entries and then recraft the text for new listings.

What About Keyword Titles?

You may be asking yourself, "What about the item's title? What keywords should I use to attract buyers to my listing? Don't I need to get those together first?" You could go this route, but there's a method to the mayhem here. First, you want to understand your customers and their needs, and then you can work backward, building the description and then zeroing in on the keywords that attract customers to your listing. It's a really economical way of quickly getting down to the nitty-gritty without glossing over important details. You could do this in the opposite order, but you might miss some very important discoveries along the way.

You're in the Marketing Business

Once you start selling on eBay with any consequence, you need to come to grips with the fact that you're in the marketing business. You're a buyer, a seller, an office manager, and a strategist, but you're also in the business of persuasion. With that realization comes a simple responsibility to connect with customers on their terms. That's where your profits are going to come from. That's how auctions get bid up and why some eBay Stores are more popular than others.

The sooner you can think of yourself as a persuader, the better. We live in a world of mind-boggling supply, where piles of useful stuff go unsold (or are sold at a loss) because nobody has the time or inclination to introduce it properly to the right audience.

A lot of people think that products sell themselves, but this simply isn't true. Products don't have worth or value until you connect them with prospects, and the only way to connect with prospects is to identify with their needs and desires. That's why it's important that you maintain an intimate knowledge of your niche.

Products don't have worth or value until you connect them with prospects, and the only way to connect with prospects is to identify with their needs and desires.

As an eBay seller, you don't have to develop new needs. But you do have to be keenly aware of the connection between product and need, and then market accordingly. The trick is to define your product accurately and place it in the context of customer needs that already exist.

Take a look at how two different eBay sellers presented what's usually considered a commodity item—soap. Here's the first description:

> You are bidding on a bar of Nautica soap. This is a new bar in cellophane wrapper with no box, as pictured below.

Another soap seller provides a bit more information:

> My rose-scented natural soap is a soft-white bar featuring the lovely Rose fragrance and is enriched with lots of moisturizing shea butter. Rose is a timeless fragrance, and this bar captures the enchanting scent of the rose bloom beautifully. Bars are fragrant, lather luxuriously, rinse clean, and are hard, long-lasting, and a delight to use. If you are looking for a premium quality, rose-scented natural soap for yourself, or as a gift for someone special, this is the ideal choice.

The first seller thinks you can just trot out a product like a pony and expect the masses to open their wallets. The other holds your hand and introduces you to a dream of moist, scented skin, and a long-lasting bar that provides delight, cleanliness, and sublime aroma. He acts like Willie Wonka, helping you understand the new life, the new "you" that will emerge in the glorious sunshine of possibility. The description even suggests giving the soap as a gift. (We'll dedicate more time to the subject of gifts near the end of this chapter.) It's not necessarily the zenith of descriptions, but it sure beats, "Yo, soap for sale." If you intend to move a lot of soap, it can pay to stand out, offer up some enticements, and develop a compelling description.

If a man is interested in buying what you have to sell, you can't tell him too much.

—Frank Irving Fletcher (famous early 20th century ad man)

Inventing Needs

It is possible to invent a need. We realize that product development is not the main pursuit of most eBay sellers. However, sometimes new needs are discovered serendipitously. Here's an example: Have you ever seen people hang CDs from fruit trees to keep the birds away? Sooner or later, we'll see a Martha Stewart–branded tree reflector that looks remarkably like a CD, retails for $5.99, and tastefully scares away fruit poachers. Maybe they already exist.

eBay sellers with a tight niche focus and a comprehensive understanding of customer needs, problems, and desires will ultimately invent new needs and deliver the products to fill them.

Selling Dreams and Benefits

When attempting to connect with the customer, forget about the product for a moment. Instead, think about what the customer is looking to get out of the exchange. When she gives you her $5, $18.95, $270, or $87,000, what is she expecting in return? How is her life going to change? What is she "dreaming" of?

When you get into this thought process, you're exploring *benefits*. The term *benefit* seems kind of ambiguous, but it can be explained fairly simply. Basically, a benefit is something that answers the age-old question "What's in it for me?"

In the offline business world, this sort of questioning leads to better advertising, better brochure copy, and ultimately more sales and higher perceived value. Essentially, you should have the same kinds of goals on eBay. Your description is part ad, part brochure, part sales transaction. Since you're never really in front of the customer physically, this is your chance to act as a retail salesperson and speak directly to the customer's needs. It's your chance to sell the dream.

Tip: If you think in terms of benefits, you can outsell most of the people who are competing against you.

Well-Crafted Benefit Messages Are All Around You

Part of this chapter was written on a laptop in a courtyard near a Pilates studio. The studio has a benefit pitch written on the window. It's a quote from Joseph H. Pilates himself: "In 10 sessions you feel better.... In 20 sessions you look better.... In 30 sessions you'll have a whole new body."

How about that! A promise, a dream, and a plan of action for achievement— all in one simple little sign on the window.

The Tivo Dream

To illustrate benefits further, let's examine a dream that's fairly new on the scene—the DVR, or digital video recorder. Most of us recognize this technology as the brand name Tivo. Technically speaking, it's no revolution, but for those who use it, it's a godsend.

The dream goes something like this: "I want to reduce my TV watching time, eliminate commercial interruptions, and avoid incessant advertising messages."

This dream is interesting, because many of us have a love-hate-fear relationship with the TV. We could take it further and say, "If you cut out 8 minutes of commercials for every 30-minute show that you watch, you'll reclaim an hour of your time every week. That's four hours every month and two days every year. You'll then spend those two days on a beach, reading about how to become wealthy by selling better on eBay." Now that's a dream!

There's some classic freedom dreaming going on here:

- Freedom to do more
- Freedom to improve
- Freedom from psychological burdens that external messages create
- Opportunity to enjoy more free time
- Opportunity to recapture some control over life
- Liberation from that dreaded idiot box

Freedom dreams are highly sought after. If you can find a way to emphasize freedom in your listings, you'll sell more products.

Selling the Sizzle

This leads us to another aspect of the dream—some marketers call it "selling the sizzle instead of the steak." Think about a car commercial, for example. The car is the steak, but the mountains, the bikini-clad babes, the breathtaking views, and the rugged terrain positively sizzle. Most buyers will use their car to go to work and pick up the kids; they'll rarely, if ever, conquer a Southwestern mesa with their new SUV. People buy based on fantasy and then hold on to the fantasy as a possibility as they haul kids around and sit in traffic.

If you think in terms of sizzle, you can get a sense of what else it is your customers want, and then move that to center stage. If you sell hip fashions, sell the dream of looking like J.Lo or Britney Spears. If you sell golf equipment, elicit the glory of adding up that low score at the 19th hole. If you sell porcelain dinnerware, create images of elegant dinner parties and timeless family feasts. Whatever you sell, there's a way to connect on a deeper level.

Perchance Not to Dream

One way to think about dreaminess is to consider what *doesn't* constitute a dream. For example, would you consider the following a dream? "I want a machine that allows me to skip over TV commercials and pause live television." There's something missing, isn't there? What's described are the *features* or *functions* that make the dream possible (which we'll cover more in the latter half of this chapter). They are certainly important parts of your description, but the benefits need to be developed first. Once you've done that, decisions about how you present and prioritize features become very easy.

> **Note:** Benefits are the springboard to a great description. They show you which features to highlight, and they give you the emotional material necessary for writing inspiring titles, headlines, and subtitles.

Fear Motivates

When considering the value of your products, pay special attention to buyers' fears. Fears also indicate benefits, and, like the aforementioned examples, they can be intimately intertwined with dreams. With Tivo, for example, customers fear advertising mind control while dreaming of convenient TV watching. With soap, they fear stinking while dreaming about attractiveness.

When you get right down to it, hundreds of thousands of successful products are associated with fears. Here are some common fears that have spawned countless products:

- "I'm afraid that a robber will break into my house." (home alarm systems)
- "I worry about my health." (health insurance)
- "My car is making funny noises and I'm afraid it will break down on a lonely country road." (auto protection services)

Think about all the information that's out there today. If your product relates to the health/diet field, you already have a huge repository of scientific (and pseudo-scientific) information to draw on. Go to Yahoo! News and search the Health category by any keyword and behold the fear. Googling can turn up all kinds of fears related virtually to any product.

10 Fundamental Keys to Persuasion

1. Be direct by abandoning adjectives and adverbs.
2. Gain buyer confidence by explaining all the facts about the item.
3. Make benefits concrete and easy for the prospect to imagine.
4. Support claims and promises with facts.
5. Keep reader interest by asking questions, presenting your product's advantages, and then answering the questions in that favorable context.
6. Describe products emotionally without overdoing it.
7. Make the prospect the center of your world using plenty of *yous*.
8. Convey expertise and offer insight.
9. Simplify and illustrate difficult concepts (sometimes with analogies).
10. Provide lots of information.

Doing It—Description Writing Basics

Now that we've established the necessity of benefits and the importance of connecting with dreams, let's drop all the theory and hypotheticals for a moment and describe your products.

Successful product descriptions do several things well. They strike up a comfortable, casual conversation; establish facts; demonstrate benefits related to those facts; ask questions and answer them; paint mental pictures; encourage further inquiry and research; and much more. The right pace, tone, and style help you sell product, too.

As you read on, keep the following in mind:

- You don't have to take all of the advice in this section. Pick a few ideas that resonate with your own wisdom and test them out.
- You don't need to be a "writer" to impart information and convince people to do things.
- Persuasive item descriptions don't necessarily lead to immediate sales. In many cases, they cultivate future business and lock in customer loyalty.

Factual Attraction

Your basic description needs to do several things, but getting the facts straight is fundamental. From day one, eBay has been encouraging sellers to provide ample and detailed facts about items for sale (an eBay tradition that would be enthusiastically welcomed in the "real world"). When you explain all the facts about the item you're selling, you gain buyer confidence.

Your first task is to list all the facts about your product, including the following:

- Name
- Model number
- Manufacturer
- Age
- Date of manufacture
- Condition and flaws
- Functionality
- Necessary accessories
- Included manuals, extras, accessories, and other items
- Sizes (be detailed; don't just say "size 8")
- Signatures
- Markings
- Limited edition numbers
- Technical specifications
- Dimensions
- Weight
- Special features/bells and whistles
- Materials (such as chrome, plastic, cotton, cast iron, wool, and so on)

Tip: Write a description as if you don't have a picture. Take a picture as if you don't have a description.

If you're selling a service—such as a typing course, translation services, or an educational kit—list all the deliverables and supporting materials in great detail. Consultations, guidelines, PDF files, and even books might accompany your service. The more you tell, the more you sell. That's a cliché for a reason.

The ads that tell the largest number of facts about the product are the ads that make the most sales.

—John Caples,
Tested Advertising Methods

Once you have your facts together, you can move on to more creative business.

Conversational Tone

A stilted, canned speech is boring. So is a bland, paint-by-number eBay description. Check out this description of a mechanical pencil set (exactly as it appeared on eBay):

> Vintage parker VP* fountain pen and mechanical pencil set in flip top box - parker VP* "very personal" pen and mechanical pencil and are color blue with satin/brushed metal caps with gold color pocket clips - nib say's parker u.s.a. 14k say's 65 on back side - nib turns and is adjustable - cap say's parker vp parker made in u.s.a. (and has a oblong circle with a arrow through it).

Your goal is to avoid this kind of approach, and write as if you're conversing around the water cooler, campfire, martini lounge, or dinner table.

If you write like you speak, you're way ahead of the game. Many of us, however, were cowed by tweed-clad English teachers and encouraged to write "fancy." We were taught that big words convey a wide array of nuance and feeling, that a rich vocabulary is one of the keys to the inner circles of prep school elitism, that each sentence must be agonized over.

In fact, the opposite is true. Numerous studies show that short words and sentences (in speech and writing) leave an impression of intelligence on the recipient of the ideas.

One way to achieve a simple, conversational tone is to pretend that you're writing a personal note or an e-mail to a friend about a cool product you've found. The method produces familiar, respectful, honest, and exaggeration-free results. Here's a good example:

> This bike was received as a trade-in at our shop. Even though it is a '99, it probably has less than 100 miles on it and was just an expensive garage ornament. In short, this bike is MINT!!

This bike is in awesome shape both mechanically and cosmetically. The **Easton Elite 7005 Aluminum** main frame is still shining beautifully with no major scratches. There is the odd small nick on it from rare use but other than that it is just like new. There isn't even any noticeable cable rub anywhere to be seen. However, the "Spice" decals on the top tube have partly peeled off (note: *not* scraped). Rocky Mountain decals have always been problematic, though, regardless of model or year.

Tip: Craft your item descriptions as if you're speaking directly to the person who is viewing your item listing and not as if you are addressing the eBay community at large.

Short, Powerful Descriptions

Once you start writing descriptions, you're going to realize that it's fun. And, just like anything fun—chocolate, roller coasters, break dancing, "South Park," or malt liquor—you'll have to moderate your activity.

Here are some guidelines:

- Read your paragraphs aloud and make sure that they're concise and moderately enthusiastic.
- Use short paragraphs, short sentences, and short words. Newscasters do this. Learn from them.
- If you tend to be long-winded, take whatever you've written and reduce it by a third. This makes useful content more prominent, reduces "noise" level, and, in this Web age, reduces scrolling.
- Refrain from using complex analogies.
- Create images, make them memorable, and keep them simple and accessible.
- Make sure you include all the important factual details.
- Use bullet points.

Specifics are more credible and more memorable than generalities.

—David Ogilvy,
Ogilvy on Advertising

Link Features and Benefits

Brevity itself is great, but the real magic happens when you combine a feature with a benefit. If you can state a feature then follow it up with a benefit (in conversational tone), *and* do it succinctly, you're on your way to extreme profitability.

Here's an example:

> With Tivo, if the phone rings, you can pause live TV and then catch up to the live broadcast later. It's great for sports, because you can pause, answer the phone, and then see everything as you catch up to live action, skipping commercials and lulls. You don't miss the call. You don't miss the game.

Here's another example from a mattress company:

> Since memory foam offers no true resistance, there is less pressure on your body, meaning less tossing and turning during the night.

These descriptions quickly transition from a feature statement to an benefit example. Some people call this a "bucket brigade" method of writing. If you have another feature to describe, you just continue the same feature/benefit pattern, like passing buckets of water hand over hand.

Basic Formatting

When you're selling in person, you need to wear shiny shoes, a crisp, white shirt, and pressed pants. On the Web, you need the equivalent in text presentation. We touched on this in Chapter 3, but it deserves revisiting. Make sure that your text is the following:

- **Left justified** Left-justified text is easy to read. Center-justified text, which is, unfortunately, quite common on eBay, makes the reader's eyes work overtime, trying to find out where to start on the left side of the page. Right-justified text has the same problem.
- **Serifed (for long descriptions)** Serif fonts (like Times New Roman) are easier on the eyes than sans-serif fonts (like Arial). Steer clear of sans-serif fonts when you're writing a long explanation or description.
- **Broken up** Start a new paragraph with every new idea you have. When you converse, you pause between ideas. The same is true with writing.
- **Typed conventionally** Don't use all capital letters, for example. They're very difficult for readers to process, and in the Web world, they mean you're YELLING!

11 Questions to Ask Yourself When Writing Descriptions

1. Is your product unique?
2. Will it save time?
3. Will it make the buyer more productive?
4. Will it help buyers relax?
5. Does it offer status?
6. Does the product help people make more money/profits?
7. Does it reduce costs or save money?
8. Will the product get the user a job? A date? More sex?
9. Is the product better than a competitive product?
10. Does it replace another product?
11. Is it a good gift idea?

Short vs. Long Copy

Is it better to go with long copy or keep it short and sweet? Short and simple copy is great for no-nonsense, "facts please" browsers. But if you go too short, you won't be able to motivate the browser one way or the other. Long is great for people who are enticed by the item and want to read more. It's also an effective way to encourage shoppers to add the item to their watch lists and come back later to get more jazzed. The approach you choose depends on the circumstances.

> *Advertisements with long copy convey the impression that you have **something important** to say, whether people read the copy or not.*
>
> *—David Ogilvy,*
> *Ogilvy on Advertising*

Estimate an Item's Value

For certain products and services, it's advisable that you set the tone of the listing and give people a bid starting point. Consider this strategy similar to making an opening offer when you're negotiating with someone. You want to indicate the higher price so bids fall within your selling comfort zone. You also want to provide a reliable reference point for people who have no idea how much a particular good costs.

Perceived value is important, too. Customers want to be sure they're getting value and not being overcharged. Some eBay sellers offer perceived value by describing how they cut out the middleman, sell direct, and avoid overhead costs.

Here's one rather detailed way of doing this:

These high-quality widgets run about $30–$40 retail, but they've been going for $25 on eBay. There's been fairly good supply lately, but that may be winding down. They come from Puerto Rico, so they're not as expensive as the French widgets that consistently sell for $3 to $4 more. There's absolutely no difference in the quality. It's just a matter of longer shipping distances from France.

There's lots of information here, and some pretty heavy selling goals are accomplished:

- Estimated price and value is established.
- Context for pricing is established.
- Quality is reinforced.
- Increasing demand and decreasing supply is implied.
- Reasons are given for the pricing information.
- Expertise in the industry is established.

You can use this kind of explanation when your item costs more than a similar item, too. In this case, you explain why the product is better (that is, higher quality, of superior design, includes more features/benefits) and then justify its higher price tag.

Estimating value helps you sell, but it also helps you get started on your description. It's a great way to start thinking about your product and considering its benefits. After all, value is comprised of benefits.

Write Effective FAQs

eBay item descriptions serve multiple purposes, one of which is to act as a retail salesperson. In a traditional retail environment, an effective salesperson takes the opportunity to present the product in the most favorable light possible. She calls attention to details, recommends uses for the object, and answers questions. On eBay, a Frequently Asked Question (FAQ) section serves the same purpose. In short, FAQs do the following:

- Dispel fears
- Overcome common objections
- Communicate benefits in the Q&A format

- Clear up nagging questions that don't fit into selling copy
- Educate less experienced prospects
- Clear up technical concepts

Let's say you sell mini-bikes, the little motorcycles that you see buzzing around suburban neighborhoods. Buyers have lots of questions about these bikes that need answering before they move forward with bids. Here are just a few:

- Do I need a motorcycle license to drive a mini-bike?
- Are they safe?
- Are riders required to wear a helmet?
- Can a regular motorcycle mechanic work on them?

Imagine how long it would take to answer every question of every prospect via e-mail. An FAQ solves the problem and gives you a new opportunity to stress benefits and reduce resistance. You also spare yourself the loss of a customer who goes to a competitor's listing to find the answer to a question.

Tip: Only one out of ten people who have a question will take the time to e-mail you. So nine others had the same question but didn't bother. If you don't address details up front and provide FAQs, you'll most likely lose those nine "invisible" customers.

Many sellers find that FAQs are much easier to write than prose-style text. The whole Q&A process really gets the creative juices flowing.

Once you've put together a compelling description for one of your products, you've got a boilerplate for other products. Click the Sell Similar button under the Action column on your My eBay page (Figure 4-1) to reuse that description wherever you need it and adjust as necessary.

The whole process is not all that daunting, especially when you have so many ways to dive in and so many techniques at your disposal to get the process going. You can

- Write FAQs
- Estimate value
- Use the bucket brigade
- Link features and benefits
- Zero in on positive factual information

Note: We'll have more tips and tricks in the "Fine-Tuning Your Descriptions" section a bit later in this chapter, and Chapter 5 goes even deeper into the persuasive approaches that work best on eBay.

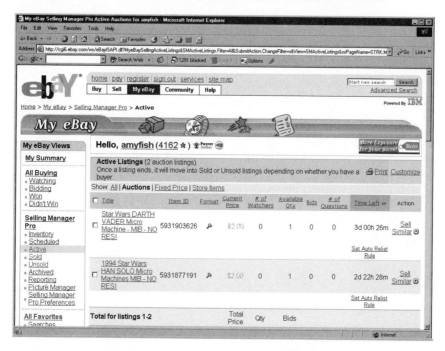

Figure 4-1 The Sell Similar hot spot to the right of each item allows you to reuse boiler-plate description information.

Bulleted and Numbered Lists

Studies show that readers like their text broken up into different formats, and they like information presented in quickly digestible chunks. You can accomplish this easily with bulleted or numbered lists, which can help you do the following:

- Communicate information efficiently
- Provide clarity
- Make salient points easy to read
- Eliminate verbosity
- Demonstrate things pointedly
- Offer information at a glance

Tip: People love Top 10 lists. Try including a section like this in your listing: "Top Ten Reasons Why My Gizmo Is Better than the Competitor's Doodad."

Keywords and Item Titles

Keywords help buyers find your product among the millions of items available on eBay. So you need to use care in choosing the words that potential customers will use to describe your product in their searches, and use them in your item title and description.

Put yourself in the prospect's place and brainstorm the words he would use to search for your product on eBay. Obviously, the primary keyword would be the object itself. Other essential keywords include:

- Manufacturer or brand name
- Model
- Style
- Color
- Material
- Country of origin (if it indicates quality or uniqueness)
- Age or year made (especially for antiques and collectibles)
- Condition (new, mint condition, and so on)
- Size
- Different spellings of the item

Zero in on the best keywords to use in your title and description by using the eBay search engine to figure out what keyword titles work well historically. Search your own keywords and see what comes up. Sort by completed item sales and by highest price first.

Tip: Recall the keyword searching tools discussed in Chapter 2? They work great for finding keywords for item titles, too.

Selecting the Right Category

Category listing is so important. Many buyers browse the categories of their interests and others perform category-specific searches. If you want them to find your goods, you need to use the right category. For some items, your category selection will be obvious. For others, you may be faced with choosing between two or more possible categories.

eBay does offer the category selector tool on the Sell Your Item form. However, this tool merely suggests possible categories without giving you any information on how sales of the item have performed in each category. The smarter way to choose your categories is to search through completed sales of similar items and examine the categories chosen for the items with the highest sales price.

For items that have the potential for multiple categories (and if it's within your profit margin to incur the additional listing fees), we offer two strategies:

- For fixed price, multiple quantity items, create separate listings for your items in different categories. It will cost you the same amount in listing fees as creating a single listing with two categories, but it gives you the power to track the customer traffic and sales success for each category.
- For *auction-format* items of unique goods, stick with a single listing. If you have only one item, then use two categories. The goal is to attract as many potential bidders as possible to the single listing. This creates a perception of scarcity, and it fosters competition that drives bidding higher. You may pay more in fees, but the final gavel price will make up for it. However, if you have multiples of that same item, then do not use two categories—the reason being you will not be able to track which of the two categories your buyers are using to find your item. List one item in your first category, and then next week try out the other category. Compare the amount of bidders/views you had for each listing. By targeting your buyers, you'll utilize your listing fees more effectively.

Also consider common misspellings or other words or names that people use to describe your product. For example, if you sell Spider-Man comic books, you want to include *Spiderman* and *Spider Man* (as well as *comix* and *comics*) in the list you create.

The final item title must be absolutely clear about what it is you are selling—in 55 characters or less (including spaces). (To demonstrate just how short that is, the previous sentence is 123 characters in length!) With just 55 characters, you need to be smart about what you choose to include. Terms like *WOW!* or *CUTE!* or *LOOK!* are used frequently by eBay sellers, but think about it before you choose such words—who's going to be searching for those words? Nobody. You are wasting valuable characters.

If you run out of keyword ideas (and you still have space—which is unlikely), become a human thesaurus. Call the product something else or use associated words that will net more searchers (think tinkerbelle, tinkerbell, and tinker bell). Perhaps Europeans refer to your product a little differently from Americans. Get into the heads of those who are typing in the search terms.

Tip: eBay searches include title only or title and description. Title only is the default and most common. This gives you two different opportunities to utilize your keywords. Be sure to include all keywords from your brainstormed list in your item description to maximize search results.

Keep in mind that titles serve two purposes: If written properly, they ensure that your items show up in keyword searches, and they encourage potential buyers to click your title when they're staring at a dozen or more similar items. If you use abbreviations like NR (No Reserve) and NIB (New in Box), for example, your items stand out. It's not enough just to get your item to show up in a keyword search. You have to dangle a carrot out there to get visitors to click.

Bad Title	*Good Title*
Better Than a Wedding Guest Book and Pen! *(Note: A lot of characters here wasted on non-search terms.)*	Personalized Wedding Guest Book White Feather Pen *(Note: Details plus associated word "feather" are provided.)*
HD Brake Light Steel Toe check out our store *(Note: What are they, and why would I check out your store if I'm not going to click on your item?)*	Harley Davidson Flame Motorcycle Boots NIB - SZ 10 *(Note: Descriptive and detailed.)*
Very Pretty and Old Montblanc Fountain Pen—LOOK! *(Note: This misses important details about the product that collectors might search.)*	1934 Montblanc No. 124 Antique Fountain Pen—14K Gold *(Note: This is more likely to attract the attention of serious collectors— who are usually serious bidders, too.)*
Fabulous Oil Painting Print—Winter Scene *(Note: This is so generalized that viewers won't be interested in clicking.)*	Thomas Kinkade Village Christmas Limited Edition Print *(Note: Viewers will know by the title what to expect when viewing—those who click are truly interested in buying.)*

Keyword Spamming and Prohibited Search Manipulation

eBay does not allow search term manipulation by maintaining specific rules about keyword usage. *Keyword spamming* means inserting lists of unrelated keywords into an item title or description so that it shows up in more searches. So while it may be tempting to pile on any keyword imaginable to attract potential buyers to your listings, it's prohibited by eBay, and it's also counterproductive to your sales. You don't need to attract throngs of people who aren't really looking to buy your product anyway.

Don't misuse brand names either—by using such terms as "Prada-esque" for a pair of shoes that look like but aren't Prada, or "like Pottery Barn" for something that's not carried by that retailer. Of course, if your item is from Pottery Barn, include that information. Hidden HTML text (hiding keyword spamming lists by using white text on a white background) is also a big no-no.

Tip: If you have a real zinger title word—one that you know people will lock into—place it as the first or last word in the item headline. These are the positions that readers notice when scanning lots of search returns.

eBay Standard Abbreviations

You should utilize eBay standard abbreviations whenever possible to conserve on character space in your item title. Many categories have specific abbreviations that are used exclusively in that field. Coin and stamp collectors have an incredibly complex system of acronyms used to describe condition. You should familiarize yourself with any category-specific abbreviations in your niche market. Here's a list of commonly used abbreviations in most eBay categories:

- **NR or No Res**   No reserve price
- **NIB**   New in box (for new items)
- **MIB**   Mint in box (for collectibles)
- **NWT**   New with tags
- **NBW**   Never been worn (clothing, shoes, and so on)

Subtitles

The recent addition of subtitles brings a new dimension to your item's visibility on eBay. For an extra fee of 50 cents, sellers have the option of adding an additional 55-character description as a subtitle. Items with a subtitle are more likely to catch the attention of browsers. The additional information is also an added enticement for viewers to click the item listing to learn more. It's another way of differentiating your product and making it stand out from the crowd.

When creating subtitles, it's important to remember that the words you use are searchable only when the buyers search by titles *and* descriptions. Remember to reserve those important keywords for the item title, and use the subtitle to describe additional features that promise to attract attention.

It's helpful to provide value-added information in subtitles, such as "free shipping," "worldwide shipping," or "100% satisfaction guaranteed." Here are a couple of good examples:

- "100% SATISFACTION **** NO RISK MONEY BACK GUARAN-TEE!!"
- "FREE SHIPPING... SEVERAL SIZES AND STYLES AVAIL-ABLE!"

The sellers had room to burn in the character count, but the added value is communicated nicely.

Creating Headlines and Subheads

Headlines and subheads are different from keyword titles. They appear in your description body, and you're not limited by character space. They allow you to add descriptive wording and enticements to your listing.

If you choose to add headlines to your product description, you want to make sure that they create a sense of urgency, offer useful information, show how your product is different from other products, and offer specifics (rather than vague claims).

Here are some good examples culled from the eBay MegaMall:

- "Save $10 and get both books, eBay 101 AND 102 for only $40.00...and FREE shipping"
- "These are the best gardening tools money can buy!"
- "Pure Indulgence! 100 % Mohair Throw Hand Knit for Luxury and Elegance."
- "It's the book that everyone is talking about—*The DaVinci Code.*"

Try some headlines like this, or keep it simple and repeat your item title as a headline.

Subheads are like headlines, but they divide your singular description into different parts, similar to how these chapters are divided into subsections using subheads. They're useful when your product has numerous separate feature groups and distinct benefits to different audiences.

Generic Headline Words That "Pop"

- Guaranteed
- Fire Sale
- Rare
- One-of-a-kind
- Final
- Close-out
- Original

Headlines of 10 words sell more merchandise than short headlines.

—David Ogilvy,
Ogilvy on Advertising

Fine-Tuning Your Descriptions

This section covers some little things that go a long way toward boosting profits. Some are good habits. If you pick them up, they'll make life easier for your customers and improve the impression you make on buyers. Others are additional guidelines that build on the information we've already established.

Eliminate Honesty from Your Copy

Don't you love it when people sprinkle the words *honestly* and *frankly* into their conversation? It sounds like rookie car salesman banter. When written in your eBay descriptions, the effect is even more disturbing. It often shows up in these forms: *in truth, truthfully, to be completely frank,* and *quite frankly.* This is supposed to sound conversational, but it ends up arousing suspicion.

On further examination, these words often point to areas in the text where the seller's confidence is lacking. Go back and purge them from your copy and try to figure out what's bothering you about the promises you're making.

Eliminate Passive Voice

Copy editing doesn't need to be an uptight, ruler-cracking, English 1A exercise. However, we do advise that you reduce the amount of passive voice in your descriptions. Try to use *active verbs* instead of *passive voice,* avoiding such phrases as "is becoming," "are always," "can be," "was thinking," "is making," "will be," and other similar phrases that include a form of the verb *to be.* Passive voice indicates a lack of confidence, introduces stiff formality, and takes more time to write because you write more words that way. Here's an example of a passive statement and an edited, stronger statement:

- *Weak/Passive:* These necklaces are becoming the most sought after items of the year.
- *Better/Active:* Everyone wants these necklaces. They top all the "must have" lists for 2005.

Passive voice usually adds another layer of code that the reader must decipher. Search for these in your descriptions, do a little rewriting, and you'll be fine.

A Word About Spelling

Avoid misspelling words, unless you're using misspellings intentionally (see "Keywords and Item Titles" earlier in the chapter and "Ain't Bad Grammar Wrong?" later). Misspellings can be interpreted by potential buyers as sloppy oversights, which could suggest that your products are sloppy oversights as well. Check your spelling against a dictionary or spell-check it with a word processor. Bear in mind that spell-checkers won't catch homonyms like hear/here or pane/pain, so personally give your text a "reality check." And if you are at all "spelling challenged," have a friend or family member check over your copy before you post it in your listing.

Caution: Studies show that buyers automatically mistrust sellers who don't spell correctly. Unless you're going for some obvious humor, don't put yourself in a hole from the start. Use the spell-check feature.

Writing/Editing Checklist

1. Write like you're talking directly to the prospect (use the word *you*).
2. Forego "style copy" and use "selling copy." Style copy is vague and moody, while selling copy is no-nonsense. It identifies needs, desires, and problems and satisfies them.
3. Support assertions with evidence and examples. Tangible, mentally vivid examples help pull readers through the text.
4. Make sure you accurately describe the item's condition.
5. Break complex sentences into shorter, clearer sentences.
6. Arouse the curiosity of the reader (rather than satisfy it).
7. Provide readers smooth transitions so they don't pause and click over to some other listing.
8. Write compelling benefits into headings and subheads.
9. Use real facts and numbers (for example, use "57 satisfied customers" instead of "dozens of satisfied customers").
10. Go back and weed out excessive adjectives.
11. Edit your copy for misspellings and grammatical errors.
12. Provide a compelling offer at the end of every description (more in Chapter 5).
13. Offer a solution. Don't waste time on theory, probability, and speculation. Good writing establishes well-defined problems and offers easily understood solutions (more in Chapter 5).
14. Avoid exaggeration.
15. Use "selling" words in your keyword title, if necessary.
16. Utilize customer comments and testimonials in your description.

Ain't Bad Grammar Wrong?

As we mentioned earlier, spelling and grammatical errors are typical no-nos. There are, however, times when a certain unpolished, ill-mannered, regressive approach can work to your advantage. For example, behold the little gem of a trucker hat shown in Figure 4-2.

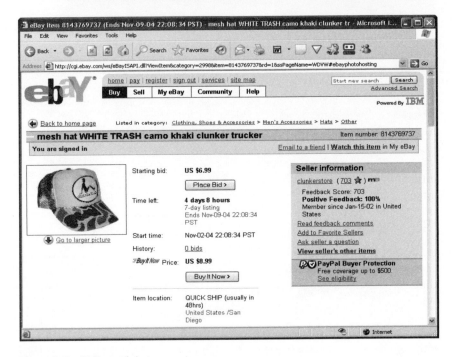

Figure 4-2　White trash hat

The description here makes our case for unsophisticated speech that works:

> In the common corner ya got the hat that everyone wears, from fancy pants in Ho'wood to ditch diggers in Des Moines...Von Dutch! In the trailer park corner ya got a killer hat at a frickin' reasonable price...WHITE HOT TRASH! Let's git ready to bid or sumthin'.

The writer captured a bit of that trashy flavor, matching the tone and style of the copy with the product itself. This kind of stuff can be fun, but be careful if you use it. If the audience doesn't get it, you can fall flat on your face and waste a listing.

On the other hand, if you come up with an approach that lots of people find humorous, clever, or outrageous, the listing can become "viral" and get e-mailed around the Internet. We discuss this more in Chapter 5.

Using Differentiation

These days, eBay searches turn up lots of everything. The listing site has ceased to be that cozy little collectible and antique trading center on the Web. To maximize bid pricing, you need to set yourself apart from the competition.

Make your wares better, faster, stronger, easier to use, automated, fancier, and trendier, and you'll put yourself ahead of the pack. If you've got the fastest laptop microprocessor on the market, yell it from the mountaintops. If you've got the slowest, tell prospects how it uses less power and conserves batteries. If your pottery is made by monks, tell them how it's sacred. If it's made by machine, highlight the perfect dimensions.

Also, remember to sell your own particular product. For example, don't convince people to buy just any antique watch. Extol the virtues of *your* antique watch. It's going to pop up on lots of searches, so you need to differentiate it and make it stand out from the crowd.

"Secret Sauce" Features vs. Technical Nonsense

Some vendors and manufacturers crave differentiation so desperately that they devise strange, incomprehensible product features. They get into all kinds of trouble describing crazy features and "XM-3000 performance statistics" that are lost on the potential customer's dream receptors.

If your product really does something different, if it's oozing with "secret sauce," then certainly highlight that. However, do it by connecting with buyer benefits and keeping it simple.

Here's a good benefit list about a Palm handheld device that was listed on eBay:

- Read and reply to your business and personal e-mail.
- Send an SMS message and collaborate quickly with colleagues.
- Type an e-mail to your team on the thumb keyboard.
- Use the phone feature to make a call and take notes at the same time.
- Edit spreadsheets, documents, and presentations on the Tungsten W handheld's crisp, high-resolution color screen.
- Keep track of calendars and contact information.

Notice the seller didn't lead with confusing features like "Motorola MC68VZ328 33 MHz Display, TFT active matrix - reflective - 16-bit (64K colors)." Those may be important when it comes time to compare the device to others, but the dream needs to be sold first.

Selling As News

When you've got new information that's topical, educational, scandalous, insightful, groundbreaking, scientifically important, or even just plain wacky, you have an opportunity to capture buyer attention.

If there is any news that pertains to your item, use it. There are so many ways to find out about the products you sell. Manufacturer sites contain news.

You can Google for new information (or try IceRocket.com, which specializes in the most up-to-date news and blog information). The news itself (like the *Wall Street Journal* or the AP wire stories in Yahoo! News) offers new findings about products, fads, health trends, advances, improvements, and other pressing information.

If the news is a breakthrough, no matter how small or seemingly insignificant, let your market know about it. If Shaquille O'Neal uses the product, let them know. If Americans consumed 4.5 million of them in 2004, let them know. If your product was involved in the creation of the largest pickle on record, by all means, let them know.

On the average, ads with news are recalled 22 percent more than those without news.

—David Ogilvy,
Ogilvy on Advertising

Using Different Styles, Tones, and Attitudes

To borrow a jingle from a weak 1980's sitcom: "It takes different strokes to move the world." People are different, they communicate in different ways, and they appreciate different presentations.

You can't sell orthopedic devices with a hip-hop sensibility. By the same token, you can't sell Gameboy cartridges with the rigid tones and attitude of a PTA parent. However, you can use tone, attitude, and style to your advantage— if you can pull it off.

On television, commercials allow the voice talent to change attitude according to the product being offered. Truck commercials, for example, usually feature gruff, low, macho men voices as the trucks splash through mud and climb across rocky terrain. Financial companies feature reasoned, seasoned voices that are supposed to instill confidence in the viewers. Lingerie commercials feature a soft, sexy, feminine voice.

Chances are, you're so involved in your industry that you're already talking the talk. If you've got the chops to make it work for you, by all means, use them. However, if you're selling Ice Cube CDs and urge prospects to "get jiggy wit it," you may have some credibility problems. The lesson here is *don't fake it.*

Nevertheless, one of the advantages to selling on eBay is that you can be anyone you want to be. With the right image overhaul, you can go from ragged to polished with just a few tweaks. For example, author Janelle did some consulting work with two brothers from New York who sold liquidation items on eBay. Their eBay listings made them look like Tony Soprano underlings selling stuff from the back of a truck—not a good thing for customers interested in customer support and purchasing security.

To shape up their listings, Janelle changed all the copy in their descriptions. No more misspellings, no grammar problems, and every *I* was changed to a *we*. These simple tweaks made the business sound like a bigger, more corporate outfit.

They originally took photos in their warehouse, with all of their equipment and pallets in the background. To clean that up, Janelle created a simple backdrop for each product shot. She also included a 100 percent money-back guarantee in all their listings.

Another client sells "stay-at-home mom" products. By adding both written and visual personality cues to her listings, she creates the image and feel of a kitchen setting, which appeals to most stay-at-home moms. Take a look at some of her phrasing and you can get a sense of it:

- "I keep your item safely in my home until it can find its way to its new home with you."
- "Please feel free to pull up a chair and let me know what you liked about our site, or if there is anything I can do to make you feel better about your purchase."
- "I choose only the best in quality for my family...and I do the same for the items I list on eBay, as you are part of my eBay family."
- "Old-fashioned customer service."

Shoppers browsing through her store get a cozy, down-home feeling when they visit, like they're eating cookies and drinking milk with the proprietor while they browse the shelves.

Connect People and Add Emotion by Suggesting Gift-Giving

By purchasing something for yourself, you satisfy your own needs. When you give a gift, you connect people and infuse emotion. That's powerful. If you're selling something that can be given as a gift (which is almost anything), you need to include some copy that persuades the reader to buy the item as a gift.

Keep it really simple—"these make great gifts"—or add some imagination—"treat your husband to the night of his life with these widgets." If you don't offer up the gift option, you may miss a sale.

Some people get distracted on eBay, and they find things that they'll almost buy. Maybe they think it's frivolous for themselves. But once their personal rolodex starts spinning, they often find someone they know who would get a kick out of the item.

If you want to delve further into the motivations of gift givers, as opposed to pure consumers, think about the information presented in the following table. You'll find the ideas and descriptions necessary to connect with gift givers.

Consumer	*Gift Giver*
Problem solver	Jokester
Needs meeter	Helper
Ego builder	Savior
Stomach filler	Educator
Safety seeker	Celebrator
	Thoughtful person
	Mr. Generosity

Recap

This chapter covers a lot of material. We got into listing organization; persuasive strategies; writing basics; tone, style and structure; FAQs; gift-giving; and much more. Don't let the volume of information overload you, though. You don't have to take every piece of advice to improve your listings. We recommend that you take a tip here and there and apply it to your listings as you see fit.

Experiment with new writing techniques. Test and witness the profitability of your efforts first hand. Practice your description writing skills. The more you do it, the easier it gets. Come back to the chapter at a later date and use some more. There's no rush. Just constantly improve your listings, and think of your business from this customer-centric, strategic perspective.

Chapter 5

Advanced Marketing Strategies: Extra-Mile Salesmanship for High-Profit Sales

---

Good salesmanship is often discredited and undervalued. A lot of people think that competent salespeople are just friendly, naturally gabby, and blessed with good looks. Some of that may be true, but most of us overlook the fact that good salespeople have well thought out, detailed marketing plans. They do their homework.

Top-notch sales professionals:

- Know what's selling and why
- Are intimately connected to their best customers
- Understand what motivates their buyers
- Are experts in their field
- Tell a good story
- Are problem solvers
- Sell complete solutions (for example, a charger and a phone rather than just a phone)
- Ask for the order constantly and close

What does this have to do with selling on eBay? Everything—salesmanship is the fundamental driver of profitability. This chapter shows you how to emulate the habits and talents of a good salesperson to boost your bottom line.

The Power of Scarcity

Perhaps the biggest motivator that drives eBay sales is *scarcity*—a salesperson's steadfast ally. People want things that are either out of their reach or potentially out of their reach. They also urgently want more of what they have less of (and sometimes hoarding ensues).

This is especially true of auction-format listings in eBay. At any given point in time, shoppers can see how many of a particular item exists on eBay and what the going rate is. If a person decides to bid on an item, he's hooked into a potential transaction in which the scarcity of the item is directly linked to the will of another bidder. If someone else wants the item as much as he does, he has to bid higher. That's the beauty of eBay...for sellers. It pits buyers in a competitive situation that oozes with feelings of scarcity...and therefore encourages buyers to bid more, more often.

How many times have you heard this: "I saw this incredible (insert name of product here) on eBay, and I wanted it so bad. But I got outbid. I wish I were watching it closer. I would have paid more than the winning bid." That item may come up on eBay again. Plenty of them may exist in the world—at prices lower than the final gavel price. Manufacturers in China may be making them by the millions this very moment. The bidding process, however, creates scarcity *in the moment*. When you bid on something you want, you start imagining how many days, hours, or minutes are left in the auction, and how long it's going to take to ship it to you if you win. You picture the item in your possession. You want to buy it now, and you want to buy it before anyone else can, as in "I want an Oompa Loompa now, Daddy!!!"

When you do win the item, you feel like you've attained something of great value—whether or not that's actually true. You've won. That's what the feeling of scarcity does on eBay. If you lose the bid, you feel like something of great value has slipped through your fingers. You've lost.

We see the scarcity phenomenon every year at the malls during Christmas. Demand spikes, supplies are low, and the mobs descend on the toy stores. You've got until Christmas Eve to buy some item, and the clock is ticking. Back in the 1980's, it was mad mayhem with Cabbage Patch dolls. And remember Furbies and Tickle Me Elmo?

The way you describe and discuss your goods in your listings can communicate the feeling of scarcity and urgency. First, however, you need to make sure there's something genuinely scarce about your products.

Caution: Don't use scarcity as an artificial ploy. If your goods have some scarce qualities to them, by all means, emphasize that. However, if your goods can be easily attained elsewhere, don't try to fake out bidders. They can make a fool of you easily by searching eBay and discovering that the item is common. The result: you lose trust and perhaps a customer forever.

How Is Your Product Scarce?

Scarcity can come in many forms. Certain watches are scarce because their production is limited. Cars become scarce when the model is discontinued. Handmade items can be scarce depending on their uniqueness. A high level of customer service you provide or the quality way you ship your products could be considered scarce in your industry. The fact that you sell on eBay might indicate scarcity in some industries, too.

This book is a scarce information resource, because it covers eBay marketing in much more depth than any other book that precedes it. If it becomes a best seller, it won't be all that scarce. However, the information itself will remain scarce to those without a copy of the book. Until other authors produce similar books, this will be the only text medium for reading these specific eBay-related concepts.

If there's a way to leverage scarcity, use it to your advantage. To establish scarcity, you need to dig deep and ask yourself, "What about my product will give customers something they can't get anywhere else?"

Loss Motivates More than Gain

We've talked a lot about benefits, and they are very important. However, here's a little secret that's emerged from psychology research, and it directly relates to scarcity: Customers desire benefits, but they are even more motivated by the prospect of losing something. That "something" could be any number of things:

- The winning bid itself.
- Freedom of choice. (For example, a lot of people buy different kinds of athletic shoes for different sports and exercise routines. They want the flexibility and the freedom of wearing the best shoe for the right occasion.)
- An opportunity. (For example, a bargain, a chance to make more money, a shot at personal improvement, or a chance to acquire some rare, coveted object.)
- An experience. (For example, tickets to sporting events, plays, and other activities.)
- An insight or educational experience. (For example, instructional CD-ROMs, classes, seminars, or "Webinars.")

You need to hammer on benefits, of course, but then supplement them with unique benefits that bidders or prospects stand to lose if they don't make an offer on your merchandise or service.

Here's an example. This is a bit of text taken from an eBay listing for a tree irrigation device: "Give your trees a hug and yourself the gift of knowing you're doing your best for your precious trees and saving time and money at the same time." There's a lot of emotion here—with the gifting and looking out for your trees pitch—but the seller also indicates that you'll spend more time and money if you water your trees without the device. The seller could have been even more forceful, saying something like, "Don't throw away precious money and waste your afternoons watering large trees. Use our device and you can get in that golf game and afford drinks at the 19th hole." If you don't have this thing, you're going to miss out on all that fun.

How to Find Scarce Goods

One way to ensure scarcity is to actually find scarce goods. Of course, you have to communicate the scarcity when you offer these goods. In many instances, however, scarce goods are recognized by their buyers. Look for scarce goods in the following places:

- On eBay
- In flea markets
- At swap meets
- From obscure manufacturers
- From major retailers (combine regular channels with your ability to predict trends, and you can buy up inventory before the trend hits, thus making it more valuable and scarce)
- From foreign suppliers
- From distributors

Note: Chapter 7 has more detailed information on sourcing inventory.

Some Scarce Goods Are Bad...But Some People Want Them Anyway

Sometimes scarcity indicates poor quality, unpopular goods. Take the 1976 AMC Pacer, for instance, shown in Figure 5-1. It's the whipping boy of 1970's cars, but the seller does something very interesting. He says, "Would be great in a video or movie." That's a great pitch—a creative way to sell an item that seems to be of limited value. This Pacer wasn't very popular as an everyday car, but when the seller suggested it as a prop for a movie, bids came flooding in.

Antiquarian books in poor condition fit this profile, too. Generally, book collectors are extremely particular when it comes to condition, and books in bad shape usually create little demand. However, if the antique book should happen to contain botanical etchings, architectural drawings, or illustrations of historic fashions, the bidding often goes higher than similar editions in pristine condition. Why is that? Interior designers and other collectors scoop up these books with relish, rip them apart, frame the illustrations, and sell them at incredibly marked up prices. A good description aggressively advertises this type of utility.

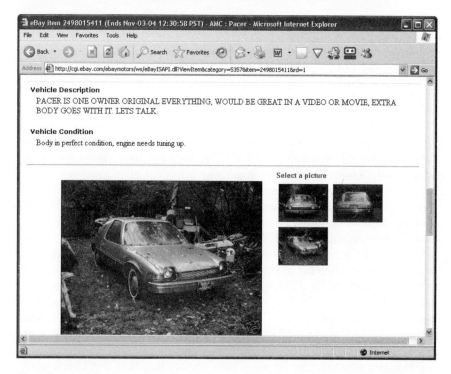

Figure 5-1 Suggesting different uses for seemingly useless items can really boost bids.

Make sure you pick categories with these concepts in mind. An antique book listed in eBay's saturated Books category has very little chance of being found. But if you list it in Antique Prints: Etchings, you open up a whole new market.

Think this way with your own listings. Don't just force your items onto one category of customer. Always keep your mind open to other possibilities.

Scarcity of Information

You can sell scarce goods, but you can raise the stakes even higher by offering scarce information about those goods. This is the ultimate marketing "double-whammy," says Dr. Robert Cialdini, esteemed researcher and author of *Influence: The Psychology of Persuasion* (Perennial Currents, 1998).

For example, let's say you're selling Chinese rugs made in a particular area of the Guangzhou Province, and you know (because you're a niche insider) that one of the weaving production centers is going to shut down because of a shortage of certain pigment dyes. You'd have to be insane not to include this information in your auction description.

By adding this information, you accomplish three things:

- You communicate the fact that these rugs are becoming scarce.
- You provide scarce information.
- You demonstrate your intimate knowledge of the Chinese rug trade.

Competition

When people understand that an item is scarce, they compete for it. Competing with other buyers is one of the few ways you can acquire something scarce, and it's one of the potent underlying drivers of eBay auction sales.

If two or more bidders are competing for your item, you'll know right away. Sometimes product competition materializes out of the blue because you stumbled on a hot trend or hard-to-find product. Other times the positioning is strategically created. If you pay attention to the concept of scarcity when you buy and describe your goods, you'll be using sound strategy and placing profitability odds in your favor. eBay statistics show that listings with at least one bid usually draw in more bids and have a higher final sales price. Once somebody bids, a "stamp of approval" is created that drives other people to bid on the item. You see this in department stores. For example, when shoppers go into a big half-yearly sale, which table do the die-hards go to first? The one with all the other rabid shoppers around it. They might not know what's on the table. There's a good chance that they don't need what's on the table. Yet they must have a crack at what's on that dang table.

> **Tip:** People also compete when items are not scarce. If your item is priced and positioned well, you can create emotional tension between two shoppers and generate the competition needed for profitability. All it takes is two bidders.

Consensus, Conformity, and Social Proof

People like to follow the trends and purchase what the group has determined to be desirable. It's a "chicken-and-egg" situation that relates to scarcity, in fact. If you ask yourself, "Did the trend come first, and then the scarcity? Or did the scarcity develop into a trend?" you may never know the answer. We do know, however, that people don't want to go out on a limb and purchase something that no one else considers valuable. That's why it's advantageous to list 47 items even if you have 50 of them. This gives the impression that people are already diving into the supplies. You can see this concept at work in brick-and-mortar supermarkets, too, where stockers stack products nicely but a few cans or oranges or whatever is obviously missing from the stack.

Most people are nudged along by consensus, conformity, and social proof. *Social proof* just means that most of us look around at the crowd and use that information when making decisions about what's right, useful, acceptable, possible, and so on.

Here's one example of social proof in marketing copy. TV advertisers often conclude their ads with the following call to action: "Operators are standing by, please call now." Others close with, "If operators are busy, please call again." Which one do you think produces more sales?

You've heard the first one a million times. The second one introduces a little twist and quite a bit more information: operators are so busy taking buyers' calls that you might need to call again. The item is so hot that they can't hire operators and upgrade the phone system fast enough. So, the second call to action does two things: it reinforces the idea that the item is scarce, and it indicates that others are actively pursuing the item.

The item is scarce, people are competing for it, and if the buyer chooses to buy, she isn't going to be getting something that everybody else doesn't want. Based on all those goodies, she'll probably be pretty happy with her decision.

The cool thing about eBay auction-format listings is that they automatically build in social proof, competition, and scarcity. The bidding action shows the potential buyer which products are most sought after. It indicates how many people want these products. If a lot of people are interested, the desired level of enthusiasm and selling activity ensues.

Leverage Your Authority and Expertise

Buyers worship authority and buy from experts they trust. Hence, establishing authority and expertise is crucial to selling on eBay. (Chapter 6 shows you how to develop trust by cultivating progressive customer-service practices. The following sections are more presentation oriented.)

Some eBay sellers are experts in their particular fields. They know their products inside and out, they offer valuable advice to prospects, and they're painfully aware of market conditions and pricing. Other sellers just sound authoritative because they know how to research topics and write compelling descriptions. Whichever boat you're in, you can still improve the way you're perceived. You can present your wares better and thus show off your expertise more effectively.

You can also fake it a little. Everyone has access to Google, and if you understand your prospects' motivations, you can focus on what matters, what keywords to use, and how to direct your prospects to additional information. It's also useful to use the "I'm not an expert, but..." approach while citing other sources.

Tip: When you position yourself as an expert, other opportunities inevitably arise. For example, if you head into Yahoo! Groups and find discussion forums within your realm of expertise, you can answer questions there and help all kinds of people. Just be sure to insert your eBay Store URL as your signature file in the bottom of your posts. This drives targeted traffic directly from the forum postings to your listings.

Be Knowledgeable and Study Your Market

There's no excuse for not providing information in a listing. You are surrounded by online bulletin boards, the eBay community itself, posted eBay items, and other eBay experts like yourself. There are also obscure Web sites that follow your industry, chat rooms and forums that your customers may frequent, and "real world" resources such as catalogs, direct mail, and retail locations. Resources are everywhere. You can even go to the old-fashioned local library and find all kinds of books about your industry.

Here's an example of how easy it is to find specific information online. We typed the words *digital camera* and *forum* into Google and found the Web site http://forums.photographyreview.com/index.php, shown in Figure 5-2. Check out the number of posts and threads presented here.

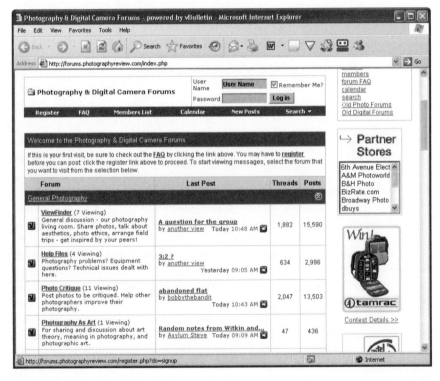

Figure 5-2 The informational resources available on this digital photography forum are truly astounding.

Tip: If you take advantage of specialty Web sites, you can answer almost any question a buyer can dream up.

If you're in the digital photography business, this one site provides access to thousands of posts by other experts like you who are recommending products and solving problems for digital photography enthusiasts. You also have access to thousands of users of digital photography products and accessories. There's so much information here that you could conduct comprehensive market studies just from the trends you see in the posts. In fact, Amazon.com returns 17,800 search results for *digital photography*—in the Books category alone!

Tip: All kinds of e-newsletters and regular newsletters are available for digital photography enthusiasts (and probably for whatever else you may be selling). Subscribe to and read these information sources.

The resources are out there. Find them and add them to your shelves, files, cabinets, stacks, inboxes, and synapses. As you learn more and build expertise, you'll be able to write better descriptions, answer questions more accurately, and offer more complete solutions to customer needs.

Answer Questions

As an eBay seller, you have numerous opportunities to add value and cultivate loyal customers by answering their questions. When you field e-mails and offer detailed answers to a wide variety of questions, you leverage your authority and develop trusting relationships with the public. You also indicate what kind of response time and what level of service customers can expect from you.

Often, questions posed by potential bidders will expose a lack of information that should have initially been included in your item description. If your item has yet to receive bids, and you still have the ability to edit the item description, be sure to rewrite the description to include answers to questions that have cropped up. Chances are that others may be wondering the same thing, and the lingering doubt could be scaring off bidders.

If it's too late to edit the description, you can accomplish the same effect by using eBay's Q&A forum feature. When you receive an e-mailed question from a potential buyer, click the eBay-sanctioned Respond Now button below the text of the question. This will display both the question and your response directly on the item listing for others to read. Not only does it convey the necessary information to interested parties, it also demonstrates to all that you are a seller responsive to your customers.

Both of these practices save you the time and hassle of answering the same questions over and over again. They also help you understand customers better and hone your description-writing skills. When you have a firm grasp of your customers' exact interests, the next descriptions you write will be that much better.

Tip: Keep a file of answers to questions commonly asked so that you can cut and paste the information into e-mail replies. Use this information to build FAQ sections for your listings and eBay Store, too.

Offer Up a Weakness, Then Establish Your Authority

A great way to gain trust while establishing authority is to point out your weaknesses first. This phenomenon has been studied exhaustively, and it works for everyone from politicians to vacuum cleaner salespeople.

You can see it at work in corporate slogans (Avis: "We're #2, But We Try Harder") and at restaurants. Many waiters offer up information about subpar dishes (that may even cost a little more) and then recommend other, less expensive dishes to establish trust and show that they're on your side. Diners who trust the waiter (especially one who seems to be acting against his self interest, which is selling higher-priced items) consistently order more food and end up with bigger tabs.

On eBay, you want to bring up your weaknesses first—get the cons out of the way—and then establish your precise advantage. Then you sell benefits or describe what the prospect has to lose if she passes on your deal. If you do the opposite, you may set yourself up for failure. You simply can't lead with a bunch of swell goodies and then say, "By the way, this thing is broken." You lose trust and sales that way. This approach works well on the About Me page or even in casual correspondence with shoppers. Here's an example: "We're not the cheapest vendor, but for a little more money you get expert advice, faster shipping, guaranteed quality, break-proof shipping materials, and a no-questions-asked return policy." This kind of value-add statement works great for art dealers and purveyors of fine glass and pottery.

Declare Yourself a Novice

There's a flip side to this whole authority discussion. If you are in fact a novice and you come clean and declare your novice stature, many bidders will salivate over your offerings and bid up the items. They'll assume that your goods are underpriced and pounce on the merchandise. Some will even try to hustle you, e-mailing you with entreaties that you sell the goods to them privately.

Ignore the temptation. With an auction-format listing and the right item, you'll come out on top. Even if you don't know the proper pricing for your goods, the market will rush to the high end when a lot of enthusiasm is present.

Tip: We don't recommend using a novice ploy to boost your listings, because when you get right down to it, most people can smell a rat fairly easily. You have far too much to gain by playing the expert role (if you are in fact an expert).

Novice to expert selling also works well because it bolsters the self-esteem of the buyer. Lots of people get "retail therapy" by researching products, expressing their intelligence level, and then purchasing.

Caution: If you declare yourself a novice, you should still describe the product as best you can. Don't be a flake and skip it. Use as much detail as possible, and describe attributes and features. Be forthcoming with the information so that potential buyers can make their own determinations.

Align Yourself with Other Experts

Part of being an authority is knowing other leaders and experts. When you're well connected, you serve customers better, and you get them the information they need quicker.

Associate with other experts who

- Share similar customers
- Offer complementary products
- Provide reviews and information about your products
- Speak to audiences about topics associated with your products
- Sell higher end or budget versions of your products (one *or* the other, of course)

When you associate with other experts, your stock appreciates exponentially. Not only do you expand your business through referrals and business-focused communication, but you broaden your own knowledge and figure out new ways to reach customers. For example, experts within your particular retail field might leap at the opportunity to sell your goods, and vice versa. Let's say you sell charm key tools, the little things that open up those popular Italian charm bracelets. If you cross-promote with vendors who sell the actual Italian charms, you gain a whole new customer contact base with minimal effort.

Start building contact networks by visiting the eBay discussion boards and chat rooms. You'll find plenty of opportunities to communicate with a wide range of experts here.

Ask Other Experts to Vouch for You

Another great way to gain authority is to have others do your boasting for you. For example, if you know an antique clock collector who thinks your eBay Store has the finest antiques, you can do the following to improve your credibility with other buyers:

1. Ask that person to refer business your way.
2. Have the collector link to your store on her site or advertise your store in her place of business or gallery.
3. Invite her to write a short review of your store, and use this review as a testimonial.

Each of these pointers flatters the clock expert and improves your business. We discuss this last piece of advice further in the following section on testimonials.

Tip: Be prepared to offer experts some value in exchange for their help. Give them special deals, promote their particular interests—do whatever it takes to win them over. You'll both gain from mutual benefits.

Testimonials: Get Past Customers to Sell Your Future Prospects

When you ask people to vouch for you, marketing pros call this a *testimonial*. You see testimonials everywhere, because they are one of the most powerful mechanisms available for convincing shoppers to commit. Movies use them in their newspaper ads as little pull quotes from longer movie reviews ("A knock-down, drag-out thrill ride!" – Jeff Noodle, Ain't Movies Grand .com.). Corporations use them to describe products ("I love the products, I feel safe using everything from this company, and I can really tell a difference in my skin. I will use Lamas beauty products for years to come. – Lisa Snedly, Somewhere, Georgia).

Potential customers want to hear how real customers talk about the product they're considering buying. The company itself can pitch all day long to little effect, but a few words from a real buyer can seal a deal.

Tip: Don't take words out of context when you post testimonials. The movie reviewer may have said, "A knock-down, drag-out thrill ride...that will leave you puking your guts out from the gratuitous violence." Also, don't succumb to the urge to write fake testimonials yourself.

On eBay, it's a good idea to take existing customer feedback and include it in the body of your listing descriptions. This way, shoppers can read testimonials about your products and the kind of services you offer without clicking your Feedback link. Your loyal customers do your selling for you, and potential customers get a glimpse into the reasons others buy from you.

Tip: You can use feedback to drive traffic to your listings by mentioning the item sold in the feedback you give to the purchaser. It's free and easy advertising. For example, write "Thank you so much for purchasing the eBay book, *Don't Throw It Away, Sell It On eBay!*" instead of "Thank you so much for your fast payment! A+++++."

Combine Positive eBay Feedback with Testimonials

Remember that most eBay browsers understand that testimonials in an item description were chosen and included by the seller, and that a feedback comment, positive or negative, is a direct quote from other customers that the seller has no power to add, revise, or delete.

Inserting glowing testimonials into the text of the description is fairly worthless if the potential buyer looks into your feedback file and finds actual buyer comments that don't correspond with the testimonials. However, the combination of testimonials with positive feedback comments to back them up will keep buyers coming back for more. If you have this combination working for you, explicitly let your customers know about it in the body of the description.

Gathering Praise

While customer feedback on eBay certainly provides testimony, you can go even further and solicit feedback from customers to use in your descriptions. If you've already established a rapport with some customers—for example, through an e-mail Q&A conversation—ask them for comments. Be up front and tell them that you're always finding out new things about your products through paying customers. They're your best resource for revealing benefits that you may not have discovered yet.

Ask these customers the following questions:

- Why did you choose my product over a competitor's?
- What specific benefits do you value most?
- How do you use my product?

- Why would you recommend my product to a friend?
- What features do you like best/use most?
- What do you think of the product's quality?

You'll find that most customers are more than happy to discuss their opinions with you. You may discover some flaws in your product or service, and that's certainly helpful. Use the positive, gushing, revealing testimonials on your description pages, though. We recommend that you place them high up in the text—right after the product has been defined sufficiently. There's nothing better than having a paying customer raving about you and your products.

If the customer happens to be another eBay seller, offer to promote her business and include a link to your page in the testimonial.

Note: There is a helpful resource online that allows sellers to copy and paste feedback into ads: F.A.M.E. (Feedback Ad Maker for eBay). F.A.M.E. grabs all the positive feedback that you've received over the past 90 days and arranges it by item description. You select the feedback you want to include in your ad, press the Copy button, and then have the HTML text to paste into your ad. F.A.M.E. can be found at http://www.platinumpowerseller.com/janelle.

The Ultimate Testimonial

The best testimonial you can receive may never make it onto your product pages. It's called a recommendation. This is where one of your customers tells one of his friends or associates that you're a fantastic vendor and that he loves your products.

At the bottom of every item page is a link that says Email This Item To A Friend. Clicking this link is one way customers can promote you and your listings. Unfortunately, you never really know when this happens (and when the recommendation results in a sale).

To make sure that customers at least consider gestures like this, include a request for a recommendation or referral in all your follow-up correspondence. For example, you could say, "Love our products (or our eBay Store)? Forward this message to a friend! They'll thank you for it." (Chapter 6 offers much more information on follow-up correspondence.)

Think about how you can generate viral buzz or word of mouth, too. If you have a stellar e-mail newsletter with a dedicated reader list, for example, ask your readers to forward it to friends in every issue. Get journalists and bloggers to write about your unique business. There are so many ways to leverage your time and get others to promote your business for you. Go through your contacts database and try to figure out who can help you. Undoubtedly, someone will be glad to promote for you.

With the advent of the Internet, marketing strategies like viral marketing have evolved. Interesting content can drive useless or even worthless products. How many times have you received a funny e-mail that's passed from friend to friend? Think about some of the crazy things that get sold on eBay. Remember the image of the Madonna on the grilled cheese sandwich? It spread like wildfire, and suddenly two pieces of Wonder bread and a slice of Velveeta sold for $25,000. Creative, interesting, or humorous content propagates exponentially. This is why it's called viral. You just need to come up with the right infectious content, and viewers will do the rest.

Storytelling Sells

Stories capture buyer attention, bring in wide ranges of audiences, and provide an engaging context for explaining almost anything. You can tell all kinds of captivating stories on eBay. They can be one line long or fill up three conventional, mythological acts. The best dramatic stories involve a dilemma, a struggle for truth or reason, and a solution.

Many typical eBay stories involve cleaning out an attic or finding a rare item at a swap meet. These are often true stories, and they reinforce the uniqueness of the item. If your products have interesting stories attached to them, especially stories that motivate shoppers, be sure to include them.

The following are five proven story formats for selling on eBay:

- Stories of product origin
- Stories of product scarcity and uniqueness
- Stories of customer life improvements
- Stories of product development, engineering, and/or production process
- Stories of artistic creation

Here's an example of telling a story, selling the dream, and selling value in a listing for rare Roman coins:

"Imagine Owning a Piece of History from the B.C. Era for Less Than TWO DOLLARS Per Coin!"..."The Romans built an empire which lasted over 500 years (from 27 B.C. to 476 A.D) and encompassed a quarter of the world. Think of all the gladiators, nobleman, and soldiers that have come into contact with these coins! Many of these coins were buried more than 1500 years ago by Roman soldiers who were going off to battle. Many did not return, and thus their money (these very coins) were left in the ground only to be discovered millenniums later by archeologists."

A story like this attracts far more bidders than one that simply says, "Please buy our coins. We think you'll find that they're nifty."

> ### Two Lessons from the Print World
>
> Here are some tips from David Ogilvy's *Ogilvy On Advertising*:
>
> - Headlines get five times the readership of body copy.
> - Body copy is seldom read by more than 10 percent of the readers of a publication (ad, brochure, data sheet, eBay copy, Web copy). *Those 10 percent are the serious prospects you're looking for.* If somebody reads all your body copy and doesn't bid, buy, or ask you a question, this may indicate an opportunity for you to improve your listing.

Setting Up/Solving a Problem

People usually don't shop because they're content. That's why one of the most effective ways to clinch a deal is to solve a problem for the buyer. Salespeople do this all the time in person. They say, "If I can solve this problem and meet your needs right now, will you buy from me today?" This is actually problem solving *plus* closing. (We'll talk more about closing toward the end of this chapter.)

The way to do this in your description is to contrast undesirable circumstances against your pie-in-the-sky solution. Set up a problem or describe a common "pain point," and then offer your product as the solution. Newspaper ads, magazine ads, direct mail, and even TV and radio ads all use this technique. Spot cleaners are the standard example—think of the vacuum cleaner salesman who throws dirt on people's carpets before vacuuming it all up using his product.

Businesses also use this technique with case studies or success stories. They interview a happy customer, write a story about how that customer was faced with painful, dramatic, confounding problems, and then show how their product solved everything specifically. They knock down the needs and problems like ducks in a shooting gallery. The story acts as both a testimonial and a success story.

Three-Step eBay Success Story Method

1. Identify the needs your product fills and the pains or challenges it resolves. (This doesn't have to be pain—it could be desire, wanting, etc.)
2. Once specific pain points are identified, flesh out what that means to the prospect (such as lost time, lost money, embarrassment, actual pain or discomfort, or social inadequacy). This step is important, so don't rush through it. As with benefits, the key to understanding product features (and what they mean) is to understand and empathize with the customer's personal dilemmas and desires.
3. Write the dream scenario that resolves each dilemma and addresses each desire.

Success stories work well when you're offering a product whose benefits aren't easily understood. A nose hair trimmer, for example, doesn't need a case study, because the functionality and benefit are implicit in the name of the device. If you were offering some new technological marvel of a nose hair trimmer, though, you might need a success story to explain just how much better it is than the old trimmers.

Here's an eBay-specific example from a description of an air purifier:

> Most people take their home's air for granted and assume it is safe, clean and breathable. According to the American Medical Association, 50% of all illness is caused or aggravated by polluted indoor air. Today's homes can contain several Organic contaminants such as bacteria, viruses and mold.... When the problem of home indoor air quality became more apparent, ultraviolet technology became the answer to effectively controlling airborne organisms inside our homes.

The description goes on to extend their UV solution.

Provide Choices

Freedom of choice is aggressively coveted by most of us—if we can't choose from among 500 different hair conditioners and 18 different apples, we feel shorted. When you offer a choice of product models in an eBay Store, you empower the buyer to "have it her way." Maybe the model with fewer bells and whistles is perfect for that particular shopper. Perhaps a range of sizes allows her the freedom to buy several for her friends. Choice takes your offerings from "this is all we've got, so take it or leave it" to "stay a while and shop around, because we've got your needs covered."

You can even offer choice in listings by posting different quantities and price points for items (refer to Chapter 2 for more on this specific topic). When you provide choices, you cast a wider net and reach more shoppers. You also show customers that you're serious about your business and want to meet their needs.

> **Tip:** People want a choice, and most gravitate to the middle. Silver coins and pins sold at the Olympic Games consistently outsell the bronze and gold ones. Medium-sized drinks outsell "child" and "mega" sizes, too. Offer your customers a choice, and you increase your chances of making the sale.

Always Be Closing (ABC)

Throughout your listings, you need to remember this mantra. Essentially, to close is to ask for commitment from the person with which you're communicating. Whether that commitment is for a sale or for some other agreement, you need it to move the game forward. The ultimate close is the one where you ask for the order (or bid).

Closing via text—in your item description or in follow-up e-mails—is not much different than face-to-face closing. Your goal is to give the prospect a reason to get off the dime and do something. The same goes for your item description. For example, you might indicate that the winning bidder will get free shipping. You could also mention that volume buys get percentage discounts. In e-mail correspondence with prospects, you can try *hard* close lines, such as, "If you click Buy It Now, I can ship it today by 5 p.m."

More subtle approaches are deemed *soft* closes, à la, "I'll check the specs. If it has the turbo booster, will you buy it?" If they say "yes," then you've gained an agreement or a verbal deal. Most people don't go back on deals, so you'll at least get a bid out of this person. You could also use language such as, "The bidding is heating up on this item, so make sure you note the time that the auction closes." That's really soft, but it gently prods the shopper toward a bidding action.

When you think about it, closing language should be everywhere in your descriptions and correspondences. Up-sells and cross-sells are a form of closing language (see the following section). Gaining agreement in e-mails nudges shoppers toward the cash register (or PayPal). Free shipping and guarantees are a form of closing.

Try out some closing strategies with your listings, and then track those that work best. You'll notice that buyers need reasons to act, and they need encouragement. If you provide both, you'll either help them move toward a purchase or you'll at least weed out "lookie-loos" who weren't serious about buying anyway.

Writing the Offer

An offer is a close of sorts. It's a proposition that either intends to close the prospect or gets him to read on. Some sellers make offers with the keywords they use in their item titles. For example, this "Star Wars" item title reads, "Code 3 Diecast X-Wing + Display Case + FREE SHIP!" In addition to stating the item for sale, it's offering a bonus case and free shipping. The deal is sweetened and the buyer is encouraged a bit.

Here's another item where the seller makes an offer in the body of the description: "Buy-It-Now And Get FREE SHIPPING And a FREE 256mb Secure Digital Memory Card Worth $90!!" This is even more explicit. It says, if you do this, we'll make it worth your while. That's a classic offer that leads to a close.

To make these kinds of offers, you need to think of something extra you can throw in to provide incentive. Can you offer any of the following?

- Expedited shipping
- Free extras (premiums)
- Lower shipping rates
- Discounts or coupons for future purchases
- Product guarantees or warranties

Most people think of prices when they think of offers: "I'll sell you 200 marbles for $18, take it or leave it." That's the classic offer. This isn't relevant in auction format sales, but it is something that applies to eBay Stores and to browsers who click the Buy It Now button. Every fixed price you see is an offer.

The key to both fixed-price offers and bonus offers is to get the prospect to take the next step. A few possible next steps include the following:

- Reading your auction description (if the offer is in the title)
- E-mailing you a question
- Clicking the Buy It Now button
- Clicking the Place Bid button

Up-sells and discounted cross-sells can certainly be a part of your offer. Think volume and complementary products.

Cross-Selling and Up-Selling

If you sell an item that works well with or complements another that was just sold, you're cross-selling. *Cross-selling* also refers to the practice of selling customers new products based on their past purchases. If you offer shoppers an incentive to spend more by, for example, offering free shipping for orders over $25 or encouraging them to consider purchasing a higher-end model or a quantity discount, you're *up-selling*. "Would you like to super-size that?" is an example of up-selling. Cross-selling—as in, "Do you want fries with that burger?"—includes up-selling, and vice versa. The bottom line is that eBay vendors who do both of these well make scads more cash than those who don't.

There are several instances where you have the opportunity to up-sell with your listings and in your eBay Store. In either format, you can place complementary product galleries below your main item. The listing shown in Figure 5-3 offers bowling shoes. Below the listing information, the seller has added, "You'll also love these items," and shows other shoes and bowling accessories. The other shoes may be an up-sell. The accessories are certainly

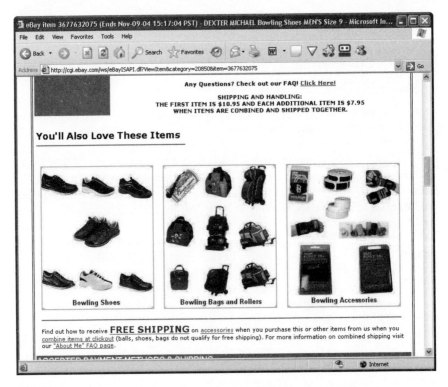

Figure 5-3   This is a good example of ambitious up-selling and cross-selling.

cross-sell items (as well as *check-stand* up-sells, which means the seller is trying to load up your cart as you approach the cash register). Notice how a free shipping up-sell is also offered. This same information is also highlighted up near the main auction item (there's no harm in repeating good deals throughout your page). And the seller has included an FAQ, too!

Think about cross-selling and up-selling when

- You carry complementary products
- Customers like the product so much, they might consider giving it as a gift
- Discounted or free shipping could encourage multiple purchases

In many instances, deluxe models are good up-sells, because the cost difference can be minimal when compared to the whole purchase price. You see this a lot with car sales. The salesperson will suggest a "limited" model and point out that it costs only $40 more monthly on the payments. "You get leather seats, satellite radio, and side air bags for only $10 dollars a week," says the salesperson. "How much do you pay for your Starbucks coffee every week, Mr. Buyer?" he asks. "This luxury model is less than $1.50 a day—less than your coffee habit," he adds. In sales circles, this price difference minimizing technique is called "reducing to the ridiculous."

The eBay Store is a great vehicle to use for accomplishing these strategies. It's the nexus of your products, where customers can browse all of your listings and these critical cross-sell and up-sell products. It's also a great single go-to URL for repeat customers.

Use eBay Functions to Up-Sell Goods

eBay has devised new ways of automating the up-selling process that make it easy for sellers to sell more to prospects and existing customers. eBay Store subscribers automatically have the cross-promotions window that reads "See More Great Items from This Seller" at the bottom of each item listing, along with gallery pictures and links to those items.

You can create default settings to automatically fill the cross-promotion links from different custom categories in your eBay Store. Select items to be pulled from the same category, or cross-promote into other store categories. For example, if you sell fine pens, you may wish to set your cross-promotion defaults for your pen sales to display links to items in your stationery category. You can also set your cross-promotion preferences to automatically sort the display of your items by price—either by highest or lowest prices. Choose to list by Price: Highest First when you want to up-sell a higher ticket item. Conversely, you may choose to list by Price: Lowest First when the item being sold has a higher price tag. Buyers are more likely to purchase an additional item at a lower price than to make two high-ticket purchases at one time.

However, eBay sellers can, and should, manually set these cross-promotions when an item being sold has a corresponding item with a direct connection to the merchandise at hand. Good choices for cross-promotions include items that are accessories to the item being sold. In addition, you can highlight items that are similar in style or function that would appeal to someone already attracted to the product being viewed.

To change your cross-selling defaults and preferences, or to set your cross-promotions manually, open the specific item listing and click the link that reads Seller: Change Your Cross-Promoted Items. This links you to an interface where you can easily select and set your cross-promotions for individual items, or manage your default preferences.

Tip: Other third-party auction management providers also offer cross-selling opportunities, such as scrolling galleries and other tools to link buyers to other goods. If you use these services, investigate the options they offer for up-selling your items.

Use HTML to Cross-Sell

If you have a product that is a natural cross-sell to another, you can insert HTML into your item description that will link the buyer from one item listing to the other with one click of the mouse. Take the example of someone who sells cell phones and accessories. In the text of the item description for particular cell phone models, the seller can insert HTML links to the applicable accessories that the seller also offers.

The HTML code to create a hotlink to another item listing is as follows (replace the words between the brackets with the appropriate information):

```
<A href="[copy and paste URL of item you wish to link to here]"
target=_blank>[insert text that you wish to appear as
the hot spot here]</A>
```

Note: For more information on inserting HTML code in your listings, see http://pages.ebay.com/help/sell/specialtysites/stores-html_-tips.html.

Automated and Customized Shipping Discounts

To help you sell multiple items, eBay makes it easy to automate shipping discounts on multiple quantity item listings. Simply plug in a shipping cost for each additional item sold in the appropriate box of the Sell Your Item form's shipping section. Or, if you use eBay's shipping calculator feature, it will automatically multiply the weight of the item by the number of items your customer purchases. Don't forget to mention your shipping discount for additional items purchased in your item description to encourage multiple purchases.

Please note that eBay can automate the shipping discount only when the customer purchases multiple items from a single listing with multiple quantities. For multiple purchases from different listings, you can still offer shipping discounts—you'll just need to adjust the shipping and handling costs manually when combining purchases of different items into a single invoice you send the buyer.

You will also need to manually recalculate the shipping costs for free shipping promotions that are conditional on a total amount of sale or a total quantity of purchases. Again, state your shipping offer clearly and visibly in your item description, such as "We are happy to combine shipping on multiple purchases to save you money" or "Buy three, and your shipping is free." Think back to the text formatting discussion in Chapter 3 and use your HTML editor to create shipping offer text that attracts the attention of potential buyers.

Moving Decisions Forward with Contrast

Customers act on drama, not subtlety. We rarely buy if a product promises only marginal improvements in our lives. Contrast is one of the most highly effective ways to communicate the benefits of change or action to potential buyers. Contrast shows you the profound impact of change relative to other situations. Try the following experiment to get a feel for the impact of contrast on your sense of touch.

Pour three buckets of water—one hot, one room temperature, and the other cold. Simultaneously place your hands into the hot and cold buckets, and then dunk them both into the room temperature bucket. Astonishing, isn't it? The room temperature water feels cold to the hot water hand, and it feels hot to the cold water hand. Contrast shows you the profound impact of change relative to other situations.

Clothing salespeople use contrast by steering buyers toward high-dollar purchases first. For example, if you want a suit and a shirt (and you offer up that information), the good salesperson focuses on the suit first so that the following shirt price seems relatively less expensive. The potential for further add-on sales is also excellent after the biggie purchase. It's the hot and cold water test: Every perception is colored by the one that precedes it.

On eBay, you can employ this tactic by offering buyers lower priced, complementary items after they've made a large purchase. Do it in the payment/shipping follow-up e-mail. You can also manually set your cross-promoted items with eBay so that links to the "go with" items will appear at the bottom of your page. Take a crack at up-selling and cross-selling with your eBay sales. It never hurts to ask shoppers to consider other options, and if you don't ask, you'll never get a shot at the upside.

Drive Traffic to Your eBay Store and Listings

eBay Stores have significantly changed the eBay landscape. Some sellers found that the new fixed-price format of the stores opened up a large new sales channel. Others saw things turned upside-down and witnessed the erosion of their auction-format profits. Overall, the way item searches turn up is certainly different. (We'll talk more about developing strategies for change in Chapter 7.)

With change comes opportunity, however. Fixed prices created some needed continuity for certain types of sellers, and many eBay sellers parlayed both the auction, fixed-price, and eBay Store formats into a symbiotic money-making juggernaut.

If you add some crafty auction techniques to a focused store promotion campaign, you can build both types of business rather quickly. Read on and learn how to play one format off of the other and crank up your business in the process.

The Number 1 Way to Boost Traffic to Your eBay Store

Your eBay auction listings offer items for sale, but they can also act as extended advertisements for your eBay Store offerings. Don't underestimate the power of this method.

Some people float "loss-leaders" in their listings and make sure that those pages contain plenty of links to and galleries of similar products that they sell in their eBay Store. You can also use links that specifically mention your store on pages. For example, if you say, "Did you know that our eBay Store is the most popular Frisbee store on eBay?" or "Visit the #1 Frisbee Store on eBay," you accomplish a couple of things: you drive traffic to your store, and you set yourself apart from the competition.

You can also create custom links that drive shoppers to your store. Don't rely only on those links that eBay automatically inserts into your pages. These are so common that they become gray background matter that browsers gloss over. Try some custom links that potential customers can click to go directly to specific categories within your eBay Store. This way, you can tie the listing closely to the category page.

Try inserting Buy-It-Now links that send the shopper directly to items in your eBay Store that are exactly like the one in the listing. Try a link to your About Me page. You never know who's going to surf where. And don't forget to insert a direct link to your general eBay Storefront. Also, remember the Custom Listing Header that you can create in your eBay Stores page. It automatically inserts links to your store and its custom pages at the top of every listing you create.

To avoid a keyword spamming bust, make your messaging advertisements into graphical links that take shoppers directly to your store. In Figure 5-4, notice the graphics on the left portion of this listing page. No keywords

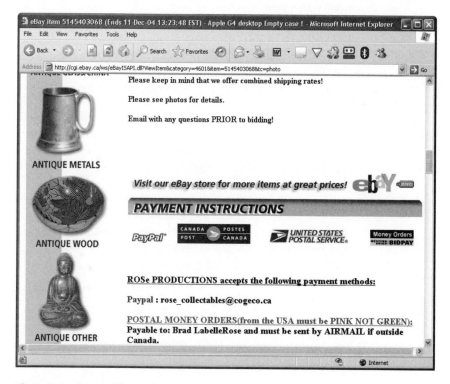

Figure 5-4   Successful use of custom links

are used here, and when the customer clicks an object, they are taken directly to a specific category in the seller's eBay Store. A horizontal graphic also encourages the shopper to visit the store.

Real-World Ways to Boost Traffic

The brick-and-mortar world is the one with the dirt on the sidewalks and the clammy-palmed handshakes. It's not a show on MTV or the glass monitor, e-mail introduction world of eBay. The real world is a great place to promote your eBay Store.

Top 6 Ways to Boost Traffic on "The Streets"

1. Make sure your eBay Store URL is printed on your business cards, letterhead, stationery, thank you notes, invoices, car bumper sticker, holiday cards, and promotional post cards. Recall our discussion of the eBay Stores referral credit from Chapter 2? Any outside links from these sources will result in a 75 percent credit off your Final Value Fees for store inventory purchased.
2. Talk up your business with anyone who is willing to listen. Uncles, grandparents, delivery people, Rotary Club poo-bahs, and parole officers should all hear about your enterprising business. Give them business cards, get their addresses (real-world and cyber), and invite them to attend your talks on digital photography (or whatever niche it is you've developed to sell goods).
3. Send prospects and former customers already on your mailing list promotional items that bear your URL and store logo/name. The usual promo items include pens, t-shirts, sticky notes, and coffee cups. You can get creative and offer more intriguing items, though, such as toys, fans, fly-swatters, CD holders, and other items.
4. Offer gift certificates. Every restaurant and many retail stores do this, so why shouldn't you? It allows customers that like what you offer to foist your wares onto their unsuspecting friends and relatives. Certificates can be created in both real-world and cyber forms.
5. Conduct seminars and informal talks about your area of expertise. If you can get press coverage, you'll expand your reach even farther.
6. Write articles for trade magazines and local papers, and submit press releases to any media outlet that might cover your type of business and customer/product profile. Don't be afraid to think big. You'd be surprised at how many newspapers, radio stations, and even TV programs are interested in fresh, interesting angles on commercial enterprises and the people who buy from them.

Store Referral Credit

The eBay Store referral code is a predetermined code added to the end of your store URL. Using this code when driving traffic into your store from outside of eBay will give you a credit of 75 percent off your Final Value Fees. The following eBay parameters apply:

- The buyer must enter your eBay Store or go to one of your store inventory listings directly from a location outside of the eBay site.
- The buyer must go to your store because of your promotion.
- The buyer's Web browser must accept *cookies* (bits of code that store information on the buyer's hard drive; many Web sites, especially those in which logins are required, store cookies on visitors' machines, so this is nothing extraordinary or new).
- The buyer must purchase the item during the same Web browser session used to enter your eBay Store.
- The item sold must be in store inventory format (regular auction listings and fixed-price listings are not applicable for store referral credit).

Note: You'll find more information at http://pages.ebay.com/storefronts/ referral-credit-steps.html.

Web-Based Traffic Boosting

The automated and connected nature of the Web lends itself to all kinds of cross-promotion and traffic-boosting opportunities. We've listed just a few of them below.

8 Surefire Ways to Boost Traffic Online

1. Submit your store link to Froogle, Google's shopping search engine. Froogle is different from Google in that its search results turn up items for sale and reviews of these items. There's none of the other chafe that comes with a standard Google search. You'll see the Froogle link on the main Google.com page. Follow the Information For Merchants link at the bottom of the page to start using the service.

2. Cross-sell and cross-promote when anyone bids on your item, when a buyer wins your item, and when a buyer views your listing from your eBay Store page. This is your chance to offer complementary products and show off items that you know these types of shoppers gravitate toward. Send shoppers to distinct categories, offer them gift certificates, and give them new buying ideas at every fork in the road.

3. Include your URL in all e-mails to anyone. The beauty of e-mail is that it can be forwarded and can take on a viral life of its own. Create custom links for certain segments of your customer base, too. If you lead them directly to new items that you know they'll dig, then you've saved them time and increased your chances for closing. Remember the store referral credit you'll get for purchases from your store.

4. Build refer-a-friend links into your pages, and reward shoppers for referring people to your store (more on tell-a-friend promotions in Chapter 6).

5. Set up reciprocal links with other eBay Store vendors who sell goods that complement your offerings. Per eBay rules, you can link up to 10 different eBay Stores on one of your custom store pages.

6. Buy some pay-per-click eBay keywords. We discussed this at length in Chapter 2. You'll be surprised at the traffic spikes.

7. Buy pay-per-click Google ad words. These offer the same advantages of eBay keywords, but you access the larger shopping/surfing universe of Googlers. These show up on the right side of the Google search returns. You can do this on Yahoo! and numerous other search engines, as well.

8. Offer online coupons. This is just one more way to draw bargain hunters into your store. Some people won't pull the trigger on a sale until they know they've got the ultimate deal. Coupons are one more way to produce that feeling. One of the best ways to do this is outlined at http://www.mystorecredit.com. In Chapter 6, we discuss this in more detail.

Optimizing Your Store for Google and Other Search Engines

The more optimized your listings and eBay Store pages, the more likely you are to rank high on Google (and Froogle) when people search for the kinds of items you carry. This drives traffic to your listings and eBay Store. Google (as well as many other popular search engines) crawls eBay and will index eBay Stores. Some people call this *spidering*. It's essentially a way of indexing the Web to make sites accessible via the search engine.

In Chapter 2, we discussed the ways that eBay submits your Store to search engines with keywords from your Store name, description, categories, and your customizable meta tags. These text elements will make your eBay

Store appear when people search for the keywords used in these fields. However, the ranking your Store receives in these search results depends on other factors such as "link popularity," "relevance," and "stickiness."

Link popularity is based on how many other sites have links to your URL—so setting up reciprocal links with other eBay Store vendors and off-eBay Web sites will boost your ranking in search results. *Relevance* refers to how much the actual content of your pages matches the keywords that are spidered by the search engines. *Stickiness* refers to the length of time users spend on your site. (Maximizing your site's content and making it interesting for your customers to browse longer helps optimize your eBay Store, too.) Efforts you make to improve these factors will improve your position in search results. Since most people only browse the first few pages of search results, it's essential that you do so if you want to bring it new customers from the Internet-at-large.

Different search engines favor different criteria when creating their search result rankings. Some weigh more heavily on stickiness, others on link popularity. They're also fairly secretive about the ways they perform their ranking, and they are continually revising the criteria they use to keep search result ranking as "natural" as possible.

Search engine optimization is both art and science—and getting into it is a bit like going down Alice in Wonderland's rabbit hole (you just go deeper and deeper!). Fortunately, resources abound to help you. Several good books have been written on search engine optimization. One recommendation is *Search Engine Advertising—Buying Your Way To the Top,* by eBay University author Catherine Seda. Web resources are particularly helpful, since they can respond more quickly to the ever-changing nature of search engines. A good, general overview of search engines can be found at http://www.searchengines.com/. Google publishes more detailed information for webmasters at http://www.google.com/webmasters/. Quite a few heavyweight optimization software packages exist, as well. WebPosition Gold is a perennial favorite.

Choosing Keywords

For our purposes, though, let's stick to some fundamentals. First you need to include keywords that describe the contents of your eBay Store in your store description. eBay provides a couple of examples of what works:

> *OK Store Description:* All the fabulous jewelry you love at great prices!
>
> *Better Store Description:* Vintage jewelry reproductions; necklaces, pendants, and rings!

(This approach was covered in Chapter 2.)

Second, choose names for your custom categories that include product keywords that you expect buyers to search on. Here are eBay's examples:

OK Custom Categories: Rings Pendants Necklaces
Better Custom Categories: Vintage Rings Rare Pendants Antique Necklaces

Finally, choose a store name that describes the products you sell:

OK Store Name: Katie's Fabulous Finds
Better Store Name: Katie's Fabulous Vintage Jewelry and Jewelry Boxes

There's so much more to cover here, but there's just not room for it all. The best supplemental information on these topics resides in the eBay Stores portion of the Community page on eBay (navigate to Community | Discussion Boards | eBay Stores to find this page). You can also explore other resources at http://searchenginewatch.com and at http://www.searchengines.com.

Caution: Try not to *keyword spam*. Your product keywords must accurately reflect what you're selling in your eBay Store. If your item comes up in an unrelated search, the customer is unlikely to buy it anyway. Why waste your effort and their time? Search engines also penalize Web site rankings if keywords are deemed not relevant to the content of the pages.

Recap

There are so many different ways to improve how you offer goods to customers and present your products in a favorable light. In summary, we covered:

- Scarcity
- How the loss of benefits motivates more than gain
- Consumer consensus and conformity
- Authority
- Testimonials
- Storytelling
- Problem solving
- Closing
- Making offers
- Cross-selling and up-selling
- Case studies
- Traffic boosting methods

Even if you just use a few of these strategies, your sales will increase because you're focused on the customer. You have clear objectives, you're communicating more clearly than most on eBay, and you're offering a variety of enticements that will turn prospects into buyers.

Get creative, and try mixing a few of these approaches. For example, you could tell a story about how one of your customers came to find your item and include a subtle testimonial quote in that narrative. Or offer an irresistible cross-sell item that moves the transaction toward closing much more rapidly.

Also, think about the larger business community that trades in complementary products. Cross-promote with trusted partner vendors. Have them drive traffic to your listings and eBay Store. Make up-sell recommendations based on unique information that you've acquired.

Now that you've read Chapters 4 and 5, go back to the book's table of contents and jot down a few of the section headers that provide information that would work well with your business. Keep the list handy and test out a few of them in your listings. You're guaranteed to stand out in a crowd of sloppy listings, and your bottom line will show it in no time.

We'll show you even more ways to pull all these techniques together and develop a plan of action as we approach the end of the book.

Chapter 6

Customer Satisfaction and Retention: The Holy Grail of eBay Sales

Good customer service makes sense—and cents. Making your current customers happy makes you money. It spares you loss of profit in sending refunds, loss of shipping fees, and loss of time wasted in such unprofitable activities. It builds the ever-important eBay feedback necessary to gain the trust of new customers. Exemplary customer service is also a strong asset in building your eBay brand. If you think of your brand as a promise that you make to your customers, good customer service is a means of honoring that promise.

The first part of this chapter will examine strategies to help you increase customer satisfaction, including how to do the following:

- Convey trustworthiness
- Create concise terms of sale
- Communicate and ship promptly
- Put personality in customer communications
- Give and receive feedback

It's equally important to recognize that customer satisfaction builds customer loyalty. Customer retention is the key to the long-term success of your business. Professional marketers understand this concept well—we see it in airline frequent flyer programs, grocery store shopping clubs, and the daily deluge of brand loyalty messages in advertisements. It's easy to incorporate the same sort of strategies into your eBay business, turning one-time shoppers into loyal customers.

The second part of this chapter outlines strategies to keep customers coming back for more, including how to

- Personalize your customer relationships
- Market to customers one-to-one

- Create newsletters and e-mail campaigns
- Use direct mail opportunities in every package you send
- Offer gifts and inspire reciprocation
- Utilize promotions and incentives for return business

Building Customer Satisfaction

The Rolling Stones were wrong. You *can* get satisfaction, and with a few simple strategies, it's easy to give it to your customers. The secret is to consider the possible drawbacks or worst-case scenarios that potential customers fear about shopping on eBay and address those issues in your customer-service practices.

Stories of customer fraud, from sellers who deliver substandard goods to those who don't deliver the goods at all, have made customers naturally suspicious of online transactions. However, once you demonstrate that you are worthy of a customer's trust, she will return to buy from you again and again. Here's how it works.

The HIT Factor: Honesty, Integrity, and Transparency

These three factors are the foundation of excellent customer relations. This might sound like a page torn from a Boy Scout manual, but these values underlie all other customer service strategies.

Honesty is important when creating your item descriptions and communicating with customers. It's important that you utilize the copywriting techniques discussed in Chapter 4 to highlight the best aspects of your merchandise and persuade the browser to become a buyer. But remember that truth-stretching and outright misrepresentation is a direct path to ticked-off customers and, ultimately, the failure of your business. Sing the praises of your merchandise, but don't try to make a silk purse from a sow's ear.

Integrity is built by establishing solid customer service policies, clearly communicating those policies, and then delivering on the promises you make. Offer your customers guarantees of your merchandise. Either give a 100 percent satisfaction guarantee, or guarantee them that the item they receive will arrive as you described it in your listing. Honor that policy should a customer wish to return an item. Happy customers are those who feel that your product (and you) live up to their expectations.

The concept of *transparency* is a little less tangible. Think of a magician who states, "There's nothing up my sleeve." Of course, he usually does have a trick up his sleeve when he says this. For your business, you want the reality of your customers' experience to match the appearance you convey. No smoke and mirrors, no tricks, no fine print—just clear and concise communication with your customers. Consider the concept of full disclosure for stock sales of publicly traded companies. They open their accounting books to public scrutiny in an effort to inspire confidence in their shareholders.

Tip: Don't think that by offering money-back guarantees you'll be sending out refunds on a daily basis. If you've described your products honestly and accurately, requests for refunds won't be common. And the trust that such guarantees inspire will generate much more money than what you may lose with the occasional refund.

If you instill the sense of absolute legitimacy in every aspect of your eBay business, you dispel the common online shopping fear of being defrauded and build the foundation for satisfied customers.

Your Policies and Terms of Sale

Along with well-written, honest, and persuasive item description copy, you must include clearly stated policies or terms of sale for effective customer service. Direct communication with your customers about your expectations of them and exactly what they can expect from you works wonders in the satisfaction department. Be thoughtful with your sales policies, word them carefully, and be sure to include information concerning the following:

- Payment types accepted
- Shipping methods and costs
- Sales tax
- Warranties and guarantees
- Return and refund policies
- Feedback
- Additional customer service policies, including timeframes for submitting payments, offers for expedited shipping, or other instructions for payment

Your terms of sale should appear in three locations:

- In the body text of each and every item description
- In the appropriate spots for shipping and payment information on the Sell Your Item form
- In your About Me page or as a customized page in your eBay Store

Tip: Use the Sell Similar link or create templates in Turbo Lister or your listing management service that include your standard terms of sale as boilerplate text that appears automatically with each listing you create.

Formatting the Text for Your Terms of Sale

When entering the boilerplate text for your terms of sale in your item descriptions and About Me or eBay Store pages, make sure your terms are easy for your customers to read. Create a subheading in larger, boldface type that reads "Terms of Sale," "Our Policies," or something similar, and then list your policies in a numbered or bulleted list. Recall the text "chunking" and list-creation techniques discussed in Chapter 3, and extend these same practices in your terms of sale to instill user-friendly readability.

Use the same font and type size for listing your terms of sale that you use in your item descriptions. Using a smaller type size can create distrust in readers as it has the appearance of "fine print." Even if your intentions are simply to save screen space, your customers may suspect that you are using this notorious trick to sneak something past them. Remember your goal of transparency and how it inspires trust.

You should also avoid using larger typeface, red lettering, or all capital letters for your terms of sale. It's the text equivalent of screaming at your customers, and no one likes to have rules and regulations screamed at them. Even though some eBay buyers simply don't read stated policies carefully, using such typefaces insults the intelligence of *every* potential customer who browses your item listings. Insulting potential customers is no way to win friends and influence people—and certainly no way to run a business.

What Do Your Terms of Sale Say About Your Business?

The demeanor you use in writing your conditions of sale reveal much about you and your business. You'd be surprised at how many sellers get this angle all wrong. Many sellers will create a laundry list of conditions of sale—"No International Bidders, No Personal Checks, Winning bidder must contact me within five days of auction close, Negative Feedback will be left for those who don't comply with terms of sale." And these are fairly mild examples; some sellers come off much worse!

Figure 6-1 shows an astoundingly nasty list of sale conditions pulled directly from a misguided eBay seller.

Although the seller may think that he is insulating himself from potential problems or customer fraud, he is also sending a message to legitimate bidders that he is an unpleasant person with whom to do business. Authoritarianism is bad salesmanship. Remember, one of the founding principles of eBay is that "people are basically good." You will scare off customers if your terms of sale seem to assume that they're attempting to defraud you.

Instead of saying, "We leave negative feedback for non-paying bidders," try something like this: "We are delighted to leave positive feedback upon completion of each transaction." Both statements imply the same result: good bidders get good feedback and bad bidders get what they probably deserve. But the two statements send different messages about the seller making the statement. It's OK to be firm with your conditions of sale. However,

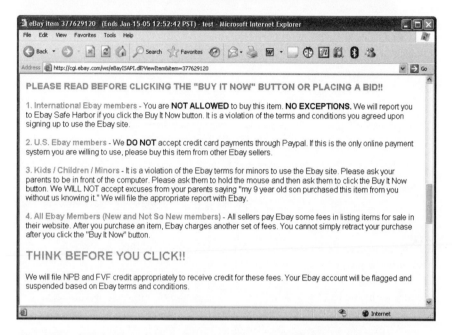

Figure 6-1 This seller's Terms of Sale are positively dictatorial. Note the screaming ALL CAPS, and if this book were printed in color, you'd see that this text is bright red.

it's equally important to phrase those conditions positively to reflect the most favorable light possible on your business.

Notes on Shipping and Handling

Resist the temptation to pad your shipping and handling costs. Most eBay buyers are knowledgeable when it comes to postage rates. They resent attempts by sellers to squeeze a few extra bucks out of them with padded S&H costs. If you charge a handling fee, be sure that it is a reasonable amount so as not to raise buyers' eyebrows when they check your S&H rates.

Some sellers proudly advertise that they charge actual postage only. This has the potential to give the seller an edge over competitors who charge inflated S&H costs. However, it also represents a lost opportunity to use a reasonable handling fee to help recoup the considerable costs involved in shipping products. Other sellers dangle the carrot of free shipping to entice buyers and build the S&H costs into the price of the product. This is a great idea, so long as it results in more sales and higher profits overall.

Determining the best S&H policy for your business requires a little experimentation and a little calculation. Examine what happens if you offer free shipping or charge actual postage only. Do your total sales increase? Do they increase enough to make up for money you could have earned by charging a reasonable handling fee? If you add a handling fee, do your total sales decrease? What if you increase or decrease the amount of the handling fee? Like all other aspects of your eBay business, making an informed assessment of your S&H policy will lead to higher margins.

If you decide to charge a handling fee, use eBay's Shipping Calculator to help disguise the costs that you're passing on to the customer. Offering the Shipping Calculator option on your listings allows buyers to calculate their own S&H costs based on their location. The calculator gives you the option of entering a flat price as a handling fee and automatically combines that amount with the actual postage. Your handling fee is discreetly bundled into the single S&H cost shown to the buyer.

Finally, maximize customer S&H satisfaction by opting not to display actual postage amounts on self-printed shipping labels. This option is offered both by the USPS/PayPal label printing service offered through eBay as well as third-party postage services such as Endicia (http://www.endicia.com). Sellers with accounts with UPS, FedEx, or other shipping companies also have the luxury of shipping goods without the actual shipping costs displayed on the label. This practice falls under the old adage of "What they don't know won't hurt them." So long as your overall S&H costs are reasonable, your customers will be happy.

Prompt Seller = Happy Customer

We mentioned that the key to customer satisfaction on eBay is to assail the drawbacks of online shopping with good customer-service policies. Another drawback you need to neutralize is the delay of gratification that customers experience when shopping on eBay.

Think about it: When you go into a brick-and-mortar store, you buy what you want and you have it in your hands immediately. It is instant gratification. That "rush" is what some people call "retail therapy," and it is a key element to customer satisfaction in the traditional retail environment. Despite all the other positive attributes of shopping on eBay, one thing that is severely lacking for customers is the aspect of instant gratification.

For this reason, promptness is a virtue for eBay sellers. Providing a quick response to questions from potential customers sends the message that you are a conscientious seller. Sending timely invoices to winning bidders makes them feel that they've made the right decision to purchase from you. Prompt notification of payments received shows buyers you're on the ball. And the pinnacle of promptness is to ship off merchandise quickly, as soon as payment is made.

Amy, one of the authors of this book, has made it a standard practice in her eBay business to ship all goods within 24 hours of receiving payment. While it occasionally makes for stressful days packing large orders of merchandise, the practice pays off nicely in customer satisfaction. Frequent feedback comments not only express delight with the merchandise, but they also include statements like "Quick! Quick! Quick!" "Shipped lickety-split!" and "Faster than a speeding bullet!" (It's always nice to be compared to Superman.)

Use Your Seller's Toolbox for Better Customer Service

Many tools are at your disposal in your Seller's Toolbox to help you interact promptly with your customers. Use the eBay links to print your own USPS or UPS shipping labels and postage, or create accounts with Endicia, FedEx, UPS, or another shipping service. It is a miraculous time (and sanity) saver and greatly expedites shipping to customers.

For prompt e-mail communication, consider using eBay's Selling Manager Pro, as discussed in Chapter 2. Information about this service is located at http://pages.ebay.com/selling_manager_pro. Figure 6-2 shows the Selling Manager e-mail interface, detailing options for automated e-mail messages.

You can set your preferences to send e-mail automatically to customers in the following situations:

- Winning Buyer Notification e-mail sent to winning buyer(s) at close of auction or Buy It Now purchase.
- Payment Reminder e-mail sent to buyer if an item remains unpaid. (You specify the number of days you wish to wait to send this.)
- Payment Received e-mail sent when payment has been received.
- Item Shipped e-mail sent when you mark sales record as shipped.
- Feedback Reminder e-mail sent if feedback has not been received. (You can also specify the number of days you wish to wait to send this e-mail.)

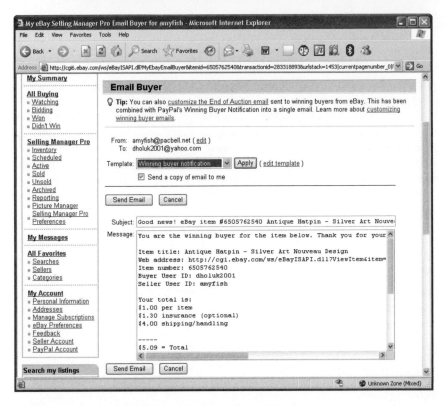

Figure 6-2 Selling Manager Pro's e-mail interface features pull-down menus with e-mail options and click-and-send efficiency to save you time and effort.

Selling Manager provides these e-mails in a template form that allows you to edit and personalize the message. The next section explains how personalizing your e-mail templates increases customer satisfaction and provides opportunities to build your brand.

A Little Personality Goes a Long Way

Another drawback for customers shopping online is that the Internet can feel a bit impersonal, isolating, and detached from reality. You can achieve the opposite effect by implementing a few simple strategies to personalize your customer interactions. Small efforts to reach out to customers in such a way can reap huge benefits in customer satisfaction.

Consider the appeal of an old-time general store, with a friendly proprietor who knows her customers by name, treats everyone with sincerity and warmth, and conducts her affairs with dignity and honesty. Retail corporations spend millions trying to cultivate the mom-and-pop vibe. This is where small businesses have a distinct advantage over their larger counterparts. If you are, in fact, a mom-and-pop–style business, that exact vibe is an easy and natural one to convey. Cultivating personalized interactions helps build your eBay brand, too. It gives your customers a solid, positive feeling about your personality and how it is reflected in your business.

A simple way to inject personality into your business is through your e-mail correspondence. If your business does a small enough volume, you may have the luxury of writing a personalized e-mail for every customer interaction. However, as soon as you begin to sell in any sort of increased capacity, you need to automate those communications while still conveying a personal and friendly demeanor. It's easier than you may think to accomplish this.

Edit E-mail Templates in Selling Manager Pro

eBay's Selling Manager Pro provides you with prefabricated e-mail messages for a variety of situations. However, the standard text provided in these messages is a bit sterile and cold. You can revise the templates to use your own voice. Simple efforts to make the text more personable greatly improve customer perceptions of your business. It also disguises the fact that you are essentially sending form letters to your customers.

You can customize your e-mail messages in a myriad of ways. To begin, click the *edit template* hotlink of Selling Manager's e-mail. Figure 6-3 shows the edit template interface. Use the pull-down Insert menus to create macros that automatically insert your customer's name, a link to the item listing, shipping calculators, and dozens of other options. Edit the text itself to convey your personality, and use a friendly tone and style. Add colloquial greetings—a cheerful "howdy" suits some sellers. Consider messages specific to seasons or holidays, such as "Warm wishes for a Happy New Year." A little flattery is always nice, too: "It's been a pleasure doing business with you" is a timeless classic.

Take some time to find your "voice," and rewrite your e-mail templates to communicate that style. Your customers will notice and appreciate the effort, and it will increase their satisfaction in your business transaction.

Tip: If you use a third-party listing management service over eBay's Selling Manager Pro, be sure to explore all options available for automating and customizing e-mail correspondence with your customers.

Create a File of Correspondence Forms

Even with automated e-mail services like those provided by Selling Manager Pro, sellers frequently encounter situations that require nonstandard correspondence. Consider situations such as questions from potential customers or specialized after-the-sale communications. For such situations not covered by the standard Selling Manager e-mail forms, you should create files of standard boilerplate text for use in other correspondence situations.

Figure 6-3 Selling Manager Pro's Edit Email Template interface allows you to customize and personalize every customer e-mail communication you send.

Don't forget that when you cut and paste text from your stored files, you should customize it to the particular customer. Again, while you're striving for ease of communication, you don't want your correspondence to come off sounding like a form letter.

Tip: Selling Manager Pro's e-mail interface also allows for the creation of one totally customizable personalized e-mail template. Use this template for situations in which you're continually repeating the same e-mail correspondence. You can also use the personalized e-mail template to create special marketing offers or cross-promotions, or to highlight your best-selling product.

Create an E-mail Signature

Every e-mail you send should have a *signature*. This is text that is automatically attached to the bottom of every message. It's the perfect place to insert pertinent contact information, deliver marketing messages, and inject a little extra personality into your correspondence. Your signature should include

- Your name
- Your e-mail address, eBay Store URL, or Web site (as clickable links)
- Your mailing address and phone number

Once you cover your basic contact information, take the opportunity to promote your business or tell your customers a little something about yourself. Recall our mission statement exercise from Chapter 1? Your e-mail signature is the perfect place to include your brand tagline. If you're offering a special promotion, use this space to let your customers know about it. Or including something as simple as "Happy customers make us happy" injects a feeling of goodwill and customer-service.

Create your e-mail signature and add it to all of your e-mail templates in Selling Manager Pro. Most e-mail servers also provide the option to add a customized signature automatically to every e-mail you send.

Tip: Don't forget about the Stores Referral Credit with 75 percent off your Final Value Fees of store inventory when buyers enter your store from outside eBay. Clicking the URL provided in your e-mail signature will qualify your buyer's purchases for the credit. The URL in your e-mail signature should include eBay's standard referral ID attached to the end. It's the text after the question mark in the sample here: http://stores.ebay.com/ *yourstorename*?refid=store. This will ensure the proper credit for your fee discounts.

Got an Annoying Customer? Try a Little Tenderness

We've all experienced them at one time or another: dumb questions, delinquent payments, "the dog ate my homework" type of excuses. Frustrating as they may be, these little annoyances are simply part of selling on eBay. So what's a seller to do? The main rule is not to lose your cool.

Author Janelle has a favorite e-mail story. She has a listing that says "FREE SHIPPING" in the title as well as in three different places in the item description. And, of course, it says $0.00 in the shipping and handling box. So what's the Number 1 question she receives about the item? Yep, you guessed it—"How much is shipping?"

While it's tempting to respond with a snide remark about the potential buyer's eyesight or offer him a "special offer" of only $5 for S&H, Janelle plays it smart and answers it straight with "Free shipping on this item is my gift to you." (This is where it comes in handy to have your file of prewritten e-mail responses.)

A little kindness does wonders for your image, and it can boost sales when your potential or existing customer recognizes that you are poised and professional. An extra bit of patience can also result in compliance with payments that are overdue. Conversely, flying off the handle, sending off terse or unkind e-mails, or threatening negative feedback will not inspire cooperation with problem customers. Who knows? Their excuses may actually be legitimate, and you're likely to lose a customer for good.

Of course, we're not suggesting that you be a doormat to every deadbeat bidder or clueless newbie who comes your way. For the clueless newbies, it helps to bear in mind that we were all once wet behind the eBay ears. Take a bit of time to hold the customer's hand through the process. Leave him feedback that welcomes him to the eBay community. You may create a customer for life. And for the difficult customers, be reasonable but firm. Communicate cordially, but be direct. Remember that in business, it's better to be rich than to be right. The occasional biting of your tongue and exercise of patience can result in more money in your pocket.

Building Positive Feedback

If you follow the customer-service guidelines provided in this chapter, getting good feedback will come naturally. Accurate descriptions, good seller communication, and fast shipping at reasonable rates are the most common reasons for positive feedback. Make these practices part of your customer service and an exemplary feedback rating will be yours.

Nevertheless, you can use a few strategies to help the process along:

- *Giving good feedback is the best way to get it.* If a buyer sends you a payment, then she has fulfilled her end of the deal. Leave her good feedback and do it promptly after her payment is confirmed.
- *Don't wait around to see what kind of feedback your buyers leave for you.* They may be doing the exact same thing with you, and you'll find yourself in a feedback stand-off. Remember, it's only a feedback comment and not pistols at high noon. Besides, following up with such a petty pursuit is a colossal time waster. Your efforts are much better spent insuring the satisfaction of your customers and selling more merchandise.
- *Send your buyers gentle reminders to leave you feedback.* This can take the form of a note included in the package or an e-mail sent after the item

has been shipped. Even a simple statement like "Your positive feedback is greatly appreciated" can suffice. Also include the invitation to contact you if the buyer is dissatisfied with your merchandise. Ask him for the opportunity to make it right.

- *Leave negative feedback with caution.* Use it only when you've exhausted all options to complete the transaction. Word your negative feedback carefully and professionally. Remember that your user ID is attached to feedback comments you leave for others. Avoid emotional responses and stick to the facts—it reflects your professionalism.
- *Don't obsess about feedback.* Simply do right by your customers and they will do right by you. Your feedback rating will reflect their satisfaction.

Tip: If you choose to leave negative feedback for a deadbeat bidder, remember also to report the unpaid item to eBay. Doing so will not only provide you with a refund of the Final Value Fee, but it also helps to sort out the "bad apples" from the eBay barrel. Further explanation of the unpaid bidder policy and links to file for fee refunds are located at http://pages.ebay .com/help/policies/unpaid-item.html.

What If I Get a Negative Feedback Comment?

Remain calm. A negative feedback comment is not the end of the world; sometimes it is just part of doing business. You can't please everyone all the time—but that doesn't mean you can't do anything about it.

First, contact the buyer directly and ask her how you can remedy the problem. If a reasonable solution can be met, fix the problem as soon as possible. Then ask if she will participate in eBay's Mutual Feedback Withdrawal program, located at http://feedback.ebay.com/ws/eBayISAPI.dll?MFWRequest.

If a solution cannot be reached, go to your Feedback Forum page and enter a reply to the customer's feedback comment that explains the situation. Be calm and professional in your response. Other customers will see what you've written. Lashing out in response to a negative feedback comment will only make you look bad.

Most importantly, treat negative feedback as a learning experience. Identify the source of your customer's dissatisfaction and learn from your mistakes. If such a situation arises again, be sure to handle the situation more adeptly to avoid negative feedback from future customers.

Remember, while one negative feedback comment isn't the end of the world, too many negative feedbacks can wreak havoc on your reputation. Every tenth of a percent that is less than 100 percent positive on your feedback rating chips away at customer confidence and thus eats away at your profits. Plus, PowerSellers must always bear in mind the requirement of 98 percent positive feedback to maintain their status.

Gold-Star Customer Service Ideas

Some sellers really go the extra mile to provide gold-star service to their customers. Get creative and find some unique and thoughtful ways that you can extend value-added services to the merchandise you sell. Be sure to include text detailing these special services in your listings—it can help persuade browsers into becoming buyers. Let browsers know exactly how great your customer service is by touting it in your item descriptions. And like your terms of sale, this information should be created as boilerplate text and added to each item you list.

The following is a list of ideas for extra-mile customer service (some of these have been mentioned earlier, but they're such great ideas, they bear repeating):

- **Gift services** Free gift wrap and gift cards, plus drop-shipping to a gift recipient's address give buyers added incentive to buy your goods as gifts for others.
- **Money-back guarantees** Buyers will spend more readily and confidently when you guarantee your products and services.
- **Warranties** If you sell consumer electronics, consider offering your customer a warranty of your goods to inspire confidence. eBay now offers warranty services free for sellers. More information is available at http://pages.ebay.com/help/warranty/seller_overview.html.
- **Shipping options** Give your customers a choice of shipping options and prices. Expedited and overnight mail are great for those who need an item in a hurry. Ground services are perfect for those who want to save money. The key is to offer buyers every option available and let them choose for themselves.
- **Payment options** Offer a variety of payment options to make it easy for your customers to pay you. eBay's business relationship with PayPal makes it ultra-easy to integrate PayPal's service into your business. Consider using your own merchant services to process credit card payments, or accept payments through alternative services such as BidPay. Determine your own policy on

accepting personal checks. Again, the more options you can offer, the happier your customers will be.

- **International shipping**   While selling internationally comes with some additional efforts and risks, there's a world full of customers waiting for your goods.

Customer Service and Your Employees

If you run your eBay business alone, it's easy to monitor your own customer service activities. If you have employees, it is absolutely crucial that you develop a system that guides them in extending your standards of service to every customer they assist.

To accomplish this, you need to create written protocols to establish your customer service practices. Give your employees proper training in customer service techniques that includes hypothetical situations and solutions. Consider a day's retreat, or treat them to lunch to discuss customer service issues. Communicate your business practices and values at every chance you get.

Customer service is a big part of building your brand, and your employees are part of your brand team. Choose your team members wisely and coach them well. Then allow them to perform your business's customer interactions with grace and genuineness. Let them display their own talents, skills, and ideas. Consider profit-sharing or other incentives so that your customers' satisfaction and your overall business success is also in their self-interest. Finally, model the kind of behavior that you would like them to use with your customers. Treat them with dignity and respect and they will extend that courtesy to your customers.

Customer Retention: Strategies to Keep Them Coming Back

Now that we've covered the basics of good customer service on eBay, we can get to the true benefit of those efforts. That is, with a few simple strategies you can turn happy, satisfied customers into repeat, loyal customers. We mentioned earlier that customer retention is the key to the long-term success of your business. Why is that so? Well, what better customer to be the target of your marketing efforts than one who has bought from you in the past, who enjoys your products, and who knows firsthand that you deserve your reputation as an outstanding seller? Selling to them is so much easier than continually drumming up new business prospects.

In most businesses, 20 percent of your customers are responsible for 80 percent of your sales. Your existing customer base is four to five times more likely to buy from you than a "cold" market customer—and the "lifetime value" of these customers is one of the greatest assets of your business.

Marketing pros have identified the behaviors of a repeat customer as an elliptical "customer life cycle." For an eBay shopper who returns to shop some more, their life cycle would look something like that shown in Figure 6-4.

Figure 6-4 The eBay customer life cycle shows all stages of an eBay purchase and the path to return as a repeat customer.

The crucial element on this ellipse is "Seller offers impetus to return." If you do nothing at this point to inspire the customer's return, he may do nothing also, and you have yourself a one-time buyer. However, if you offer the customer new deals, promotions, or other incentives to return to your store, he will begin the cycle anew. If you can get him to roll through the cycle again and again, you've discovered the art of customer retention. Master it, and you might as well be printing your own money. This section uncovers tricks of the trade that work as catalysts to reel customers back to buy more.

Personalized Customer Interactions—Part Deux

Let's return to the discussion of the old general store proprietor—the one who greets all customers by name and treats them with sincerity and warmth. This smart business owner would also provide her customers with better service by learning their personal characteristics, shopping preferences, and purchasing needs. In doing so, she also ensures her financial success by generating more sales from her loyal customers. eBay sellers can use similar customer relations tactics to keep customers coming back for more.

One-to-One Marketing

The Web revolutionized the old general store business model. Its interactivity allows for many individualized selling opportunities. Marketing pros call this *one-to-one marketing*. Think of the possibilities provided by database technologies and software to manage direct sales from proprietor to customer. eBay itself is a marvel of this new technology.

The first step for eBay sellers to tap into this lucrative tactic is to identify the relationship that your customers have with your products. For example, if you sell items that will eventually need to be replenished, you have a built-in opportunity for repeat business. Beauty products and cosmetics, printer cartridges, supplies for crafts or hobbies—all these items become depleted and need to be replaced. The key is to get your customers to return to you for the replenishing.

Conversely, if you specialize in scarce items such as antiques and collectibles, parts for project cars, hot fashions, or other difficult to find goods, you can create a customer "wish list." Imagine having a buyer lined up for an item before you even put it up for sale—or even better, having two prospects who will bid against each other!

Finally, if you forge your brand identity in the minds of your customers, offer them desirable merchandise, and give excellent customer service, they will return to you for the pure pleasure of shopping at your eBay Store.

Managing Customer Data and Contact Information

Before we dive into specific examples of ways to drum up repeat business, you need to strategize the way you manage your customers, their interests and shopping patterns, and their contact information. If you don't have this data in an organized and easily accessible format, your efforts will be more time consuming and may not yield substantial results.

Small-volume businesses with modest customer bases can manage such marketing efforts on an individual basis. It's as easy as creating a spreadsheet that holds your customer contact information, their purchases, and their preferences and wishes.

If you deal in large volume, it's wise to bunch your customers into groups to target your one-to-one marketing efforts. They can be grouped by their frequency of visits to your store or by the type of products they purchase. Group your loyal customers, and then focus your remaining efforts on customers most likely to yield results. One-time buyers with multiple purchases or with high-ticket purchases are smart places to start. However, if your time and resources allow, pursue each and every customer with your retention efforts, no matter how large or small their purchases. They key is to always have fresh prospects.

Tools to Help You Manage Customer Contact Data

Many sellers use Outlook Express to manage e-mail groups by customer types to consolidate efforts. Or you can consider investing in customer management software like ACT! (http://www.act.com), which functions like Outlook Express on steroids to help you manage your customer interactions. Other services such as 1ShoppingCart (http://www.oneshoppingcart.com) offer sellers powerful e-mail marketing management tools along with their other e-commerce services.

There's also software specifically designed for creating e-mail groups for eBay sellers. HammerTap's Bay Mail Pro allows you create an address book of eBay users and send bulk e-mails to specified groups within your address book. You can create mailing lists and e-mail templates, and you only have to plug in the eBay user ID, because the software automatically looks up the e-mail addresses for you. More information is available at http://www .hammertap.com/baymailpro.

If your business moves a ton of product and you have a huge customer base, you may consider investing in heavy-duty customer relationship management software. Companies such as Siebel (http://www.siebel.com) offer customized software to assist retail businesses in managing a high volume of customers and their buying activities.

Later in this chapter in the section "eBay Stores E-mail Marketing Program," we will discuss a new e-mail program offered by eBay that makes managing groups of customers for retention marketing easy. It also simplifies the opt-in process, a subject we'll discuss next.

Opting In

A major caveat to the one-to-one and direct marketing suggestions in this chapter is that, per eBay policy, you must first obtain permission from your customers to participate in marketing activities that involve them. Customers are much more receptive to marketing materials that they've agreed to receive.

In Internet-speak, this is called allowing your customers to "opt-in." With their permission in place, any e-mail promotion, newsletter, or other ad campaign will be a welcome item in their inbox. Without their permission, they'll view your promotional material as spam, click the Delete button, and won't return to shop with you again.

Getting customers to opt-in to your retention efforts is as simple as just asking. Include an invitation to receive marketing materials from you in the e-mail correspondence you send. Use the Selling Manager Pro e-mail template editing capability discussed earlier to include an invitation to opt-in to your promotional offers.

Note that it is against eBay's policy to send marketing e-mails to your customers once you have completed the post-sale e-mail process, unless your customers have opted-in to receive further communications from you. Design your own opt-in process with your customer e-mails, or use the system offered by the eBay Email Marketing Program, but be sure to get your customers A-OK before launching any retention efforts.

Caution: eBay requires that sellers obtain opt-in permission from customers to include them in marketing and e-mail campaigns. Use Selling Manager Pro's e-mail template editing feature to include an opt-in invitation in every correspondence you send out.

Newsletter Mojo

Creating a free newsletter with insider information and educational material about your niche can pump up sales handsomely. Valuable information about your products and your business is like a gift to your customers, and it's a gift that gives back to you. It draws them back to your business, it piques their interest in your products, and it encourages them to purchase more from you. It's a highly profitable endeavor that creates a reciprocal relationship—you give them information and they give you their business.

Don't think of a newsletter as a way to overwhelm your customers and prospects with advertising, though. It's just a way to establish a dialog with your audience. Use the medium to help customers learn more about your industry and the uses for your products. Make it practical and down to earth. Forget about overt pitches and heavy-handed marketing speak. You can also initiate a dialog in which you ask customers about their needs or conduct polls.

When you write newsletters that provide valuable information, your readers learn more about your business, and you do, too!

What to Include in a Newsletter

The Number 1 rule for newsletter writing is *be informative*. If you're going to spend the time writing a newsletter, you need to come up with information that is interesting to your customers. So what works? Here's a short list:

- Sale information
- Upcoming events (at your eBay Store or in the physical world)
- New merchandise and expansion of product lines
- Inside information concerning seasonal trends or supply issues
- New developments in the industry
- News about famous people who use your product or service
- Testimonial stories from reputable sources
- Certifications or awards granted to your business (relate this to customer value)

- New or novel ways to use your product (think of Avon's 50 uses for its Skin-So-Soft product)
- News about your product that has surfaced on local or national news programs

Remember, news is the crucial element in a newsletter. Don't tell people things they already know, and don't repeat content from your eBay Store, item listings, or About Me page. Get creative: if you sell culinary tools, include an uncommon recipe; if you sell baby toys, include information on early childhood development. Include information that is interesting on its own but also encourages the sale of your merchandise.

Once you've offered valuable or interesting information to your customer, give a little marketing push in your newsletter. Always include a link to your eBay Store and an incentive to return. It can be a 10-percent-off coupon, free shipping offers, or information about current and future listings. Offer them a great reason to return to your store.

In your newsletter, always include a link to your eBay Store and an incentive to return. It can be a 10-percent-off coupon, free shipping offers, or information about current and future listings. Offer them a great reason to return to your store.

Keep your newsletter short and sweet with no articles longer than 200 words. Think chunks and sound bites here. Keep the tone personal and familiar, and write as if you're speaking to your customers directly. Pay attention to headlines—go back and reread the Chapter 4 discussion on headlines if you need to. The same rules apply, except that newsletter headlines are more informational and news focused.

Discovering and Developing Brand with a Newsletter

Newsletters show your audience the mindset, personality, needs, and aspirations of your organization and its brand. It's unlike the copy you create in your item descriptions that serves the purpose of selling a product. In a newsletter, it's much easier to come out and say things without creative constraints. When your customers and prospects know "where you're coming from," they gain another level of personal association with regard to your business. Customers let their guard down a little and they feel like they're engaging with an acquaintance rather than a big, sterile company.

No matter what business you're in, creating a newsletter is an exercise in understanding the value of your business and finding ways to communicate that to your audience. It's another way to get your marketing brain chugging along. Writing reinforces the things you learn. It serves the dual purpose of conveying your brand to your customers while helping you continually refine your brand image.

eBay Stores E-mail Marketing Program

eBay now offers sellers an extremely simple way to create marketing newsletters and send them to customers. With the eBay Stores E-mail Marketing Program, sellers create customized e-mails or newsletters to send to customers. The e-mail campaigns can include featured items with pictures, lists of items currently available in your store, and text with personalized messages, articles, or any other element you wish to include.

You can edit existing templates provided by eBay (which can be customized with your own header) or plug in your own HTML. Either way, your e-mail newsletter is delivered with links directly to your store and listings for ease of shopping. Figure 6-5 shows a sample of a newsletter created with the program. Note the niche focus of the subject, the eBay Stores URL link at the top, the article that interests the photo-collector recipient, and the gallery photo links to purchase goods currently for sale.

The program also allows you to create five different newsletters with five different mailing lists. Remember the customer groups we discussed earlier? This is an excellent opportunity to tailor different newsletters to appeal to different types of buyers.

eBay makes it easy to get customers to opt-in to your newsletter mailings and build your mailing lists. Encourage your buyers to add your eBay Store to their favorite sellers and stores list. The link automatically appears at the top of your eBay Store pages. You should also insert a link in all of your item listings. Use the Inserts pull-down menu in the Description section of the Sell Your Item form to enter the HTML that inserts the link in your description text. Finally, include the link in every e-mail you send out.

When your customers click the Add To My Favorite Store button, they are linked to a page that allows them to select to opt-in to your newsletter. Include text with your link that guides your customers to click the box for the newsletters to which they want to subscribe. Figure 6-6 provides a view of this page.

With mailing lists ready to go, just create your newsletters, send them off, and wait for the business to roll in. Your e-mail campaign will also go through eBay's e-mail server, which helps avoid spam filters and cuts down on the number of undeliverable messages.

Note: eBay limits the frequency that you can send e-mail campaigns to once a week. However, this is appropriate timing for retention marketing efforts. If you flood your customers with too many marketing messages, they will be turned off from shopping with you.

ANTIQUE PHOTO COLLECTOR NEWSLETTER

Holiday Edition: December 20, 2004

Compliments of RED FISH Antiques and Collectibles

http://stores.ebay.com/RED-FISH-Antiques-and-Collectibles

This Week's Topic: Collecting Albumen Prints

What is an Albumen Print . . .

An albumen print is created from a glass negative on paper coated with egg whites. It was first introduced in 1850 and widely used from 1860 to 1890. Popularity of the albumen print waned at the turn of the 20th Century.

How to identify an Albumen Print . . .

Albumen print subjects are appropriate to the era when this process was was popular. Fortunately, the appearance of albumen prints is dramatically different that other print processes of the time: Calotypes and salt prints appear to have the image imbedded in the paper, whereas albumen prints seem to "float" on the surface. Look for shadow tones ranging from muddy brown to charcoal and a yellowing of the albumen base.

What to look for when collecting . . .

For the beginning collector, seek subjects of personal interest or aesthetic appeal. Architectural shots of homes, farms, animal and portraits abound. Just collect what "speaks to you." Albumen images in this category are usually priced between $5 to $25.

For an intermediate collector, seek albumen images depicting modes of transportation (trains and horse-drawn carriages are popular), ethnic and cultural subjects, and indentifiable towns, businesses or streets. Average price: $25 to $200.

For the deep-pocketed collector, seek works by known photographers such as Barnard, Jackson, O'Sullivan, Frith, Muybridge and others. Priced from $200 to ???!!!

Our eBay store offers a lovely array of albumen prints, along with many other 19th and early 20th century photograph processes.

Check out some of the lovely antique photos currently for sale in our store:

Item Title

 CUBAN COUNTRYSIDE - three vintage 1910s photos
US $10.00 *Buy It Now*
End Date: Jan-06-05 17:29:54 PST

 MILITARY TROOP - Circa 1910 Hand Tinted Photo
US $8.00 *Buy It Now*
End Date: Jan-12-05 15:23:45 PST

 CATHOLIC CHURCH IN IDAHO - Circa 1910 Vintage Photos
US $8.00 *Buy It Now*
End Date: Jan-12-05 16:47:16 PST

 SNOWY SCENE - Vintage Photograph circa 1920
US $8.00 *Buy It Now*
End Date: Jan-12-05 16:47:26 PST

 CORONADO HOTEL, San Diego - c. 1920 Photograph
US $6.00 *Buy It Now*
End Date: Jan-12-05 09:00:48 PST

 EASTER PAGEANT - c. 1930 Antique Photograph
US $6.00 *Buy It Now*
End Date: Jan-12-05 16:16:47 PST

 CHILDREN'S YACHT PARTY - c. 1933 Vintage Photo
US $6.00 *Buy It Now*
End Date: Jan-12-05 16:47:18 PST

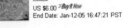 HORSEBACK THROUGH THE SIERRAS - C. 1900 Antique Photo
US $6.00 *Buy It Now*
End Date: Jan-12-05 16:47:21 PST

 SEASCAPE - Beautiful Antique Photograph c. 1920
US $6.00 *Buy It Now*
End Date: Jan-06-05 17:30:06 PST

 COWBOY! - Circa 1953 Vintage Photograph
US $5.00 *Buy It Now*
End Date: Jan-12-05 09:00:50 PST

Figure 6-5   This newsletter was created with eBay's E-mail Marketing Program.

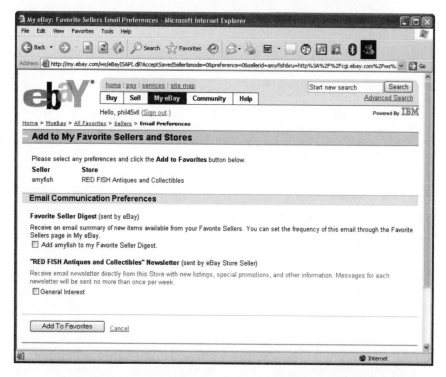

Figure 6-6   The Add To My Favorite Sellers and Store page allows customers to add themselves to your E-mail Marketing Campaign lists. It makes opting-in easy for both buyer and seller.

To sweeten the deal, eBay reports on the effectiveness of your e-mail campaigns, including the following information:

- Total number of recipients
- E-mail opened
- Item clicks
- Store clicks
- Member profile clicks (shows feedback rating and comments)
- Total number of bids and Buy It Nows the e-mail generated
- Charges incurred

eBay gives a free monthly e-mail allocation depending on the Store subscription level. The monthly allocation breaks down as follows:

- **Basic Store**   100 free e-mails a month
- **Featured Store**   1000 free e-mails a month
- **Anchor Store**   4000 free e-mails a month

Once you pass your monthly allocation, eBay will charge you one cent for each additional e-mail you send as part of your e-mail marketing campaign. This is an incredible opportunity to launch a customer retention effort for very little cost. Additional information is available at http://pages.ebay.com/ storefronts/emailmarketing.html.

> **Tip:** You may have noticed a second box on the Add To My Favorite page—the Favorite Seller Digest. Encourage buyers to add you to their Favorite Seller Digest. This gives them the option to receive a weekly, biweekly, or monthly e-mail that includes your newly listed items. While you don't have the option of customizing this digest, as you do with your own newsletter, it's still a great promotion for your store. And it costs you nothing.

Mailed vs. E-mailed Newsletters— The Great Debate

Marketing newsletters have historically been printed items sent via "snail mail." Having a simple, physical newsletter to send to your customers has its benefits for eBay selling, too. There's something special about getting mail—especially if it's nicely designed and printed and full of useful information. It sticks in the customer's mind better than an e-mail. It causes them to pause and reflect on your business. It lingers on their desktop and can be looked at repeatedly or passed on to a friend. It reinforces your brand. Plus, you don't have the worries of spam blockers preventing the delivery of your message or customers ignoring your e-mail and clicking the Delete button.

The benefit of e-mail newsletters is the interactivity they provide the customer. With links to take the customer immediately to an item for sale, it seizes customer purchase impulses in a way that a piece of snail mail can't. E-mailed newsletters are also substantially less expensive (and time consuming) than printing and mailing your newsletter.

So what's a seller to do? You can do both: create your e-mail newsletter campaign, but use the same information to create a printable version of the newsletter. Include in your printed version your eBay store URL along with information for opting-in to the e-mail version.

Consider using professional printing services to give your printed materials extra punch. Online printing services such as VistaPrint (http://www .vistaprint.com) offer preformed templates and custom-designed options for a variety of printed marketing materials, including newsletters and flyers. Many eBay users use VistaPrint for their free business card offers, and once you're on their mailing list, you'll frequently receive promotional offers that make their pay-for-print services very reasonably priced. (This is a prime example of a marketing retention effort that you can emulate!)

Given the costs involved with postage, target the mailed correspondence to a select group of customers you believe will respond most strongly.

However, print plenty of extra copies of your newsletter and include it in every package you send out.

We mentioned earlier that a newsletter is a gift of information you give to your customers. Our next section discusses how to use the power of gifts and other direct marketing efforts to retain loyal customers.

eBay Stores Promotional Flyer

A new service offered to eBay Stores subscribers is an interface where sellers can create printed promotional flyers easily. Offered are customizable templates where sellers can choose to include Store information, the Store URL, personalized messages to customers, and showcases of items for sale. You can also insert preexisting Store settings such as your policies or promotional boxes. This service is free of charge, and is a simple way to print a newsletter-style flyer that can be mailed directly to customers, placed in packages, or distributed as one would pass out business cards. The link to create an eBay Store Promotional Flyer is available on the Manage Your Store page. More information is available at: http://pages.ebay.com/help/specialtysites/promotional-flyer-ov.html.

Direct Marketing

Advertising at the point of purchase just makes sense, period. Remember our cross-selling and up-selling discussion from Chapter 5? Encourage multiple purchases when a customer buys something from you. Use the cross-promotions on your item listings to your best advantage. Take the opportunity in your confirmation e-mails to suggest a go-along item. Offer shipping discounts for multiple purchases. Encourage your customers to visit your store again.

Every package you send out is a unique direct marketing opportunity. Think of traditional marketers and junk mail. How much money and effort (and trees) do they waste sending out tons of stuff every day? Our mailboxes are clogged with it. But putting an extra marketing item in each package you send is simple. And the target is your ideal demographic: a paying customer who is excited to open his eBay package!

Suggestions for marketing materials that can be dropped in each package include the following:

- A printed copy of your newsletter or eBay Store Promotional Flyer
- Your business card

- Catalogs/brochures
- A thank you note on your business stationery (including a gentle request for positive feedback)
- Coupons that encourage repeat business (for example, a discount or free shipping on a next order)
- A gift as a token of appreciation

Tip: Don't forget to display your eBay Store URL prominently on every item you include in your packages. Make it as simple as possible for your customers to return to your store.

The Power of Reciprocation: Why Freebies Increase Sales

If you give, you will receive. This not just a religious homily; it's a psychological fact that operates in every culture on the planet. The phenomenon is discussed at length in Robert B. Cialdini's *Influence: The Psychology of Persuasion* (1998), with statistical studies to back it up. If you're interested in the psychology involved, pick up a copy and delve deeper.

Reciprocation is built into our societal code of ethics, our culture, and our collective behavioral systems. People reciprocate when they are given a gift. It doesn't matter whether they like or don't like the gift or the giver; they feel an obligation to reciprocate.

You may say, "Hey, that's not me. I don't feel obligated to reciprocate." You may eat the cheese at the supermarket freebie station and pass on purchasing. You may receive personalized address labels from the American Heart Association, actually use them, and toss the donation card into the garbage. It's probably because you recognize and analyze the marketing concepts at work and second-guess your impulses.

Most people do reciprocate, though. On impulse, we're trained to reciprocate and feel guilt and shame when we don't live up to that contract. Giving back provides closure when we've been given a gift.

You can really see the power of the contract in action when you try to return or refuse a gift. Have you ever been given a gift and then decided to give it back after accepting it? You usually don't give it back because you don't want it or you can't use it; you give it back *because you don't want to be bound by the reciprocation contract.* You don't want to be obligated to the exchange relationship. When you accept gifts, you accept the reciprocation obligation. This is where the phrase "much obliged" comes from.

eBay does have some restrictions about selling gifts as part of a listing (see "eBay's Rules Concerning Advertising Gifts" for an explanation). However, you can certainly slip a gift into the package you ship. When you do this, make sure that you give a reason for the gift that indicates your expectation from the customer. This could be anything from "remember me the next time you purchase" to "please e-mail your friends and tell them what a great deal you got."

Here's a real-life eBay example. A ticket broker who specialized in concerts slipped a free six-pack of Coronas and limes into each of his Jimmy Buffet ticket shipments. How did he do it? He included a $10 gift certificate to a local supermarket chain in each envelope.

Tip: Consider investing in promotional gifts that are custom printed with your business name, contact information, and eBay Store URL. Items such as printed pens, key rings, magnets, notepads, and other novelties are inexpensive when ordered in bulk and deliver the message of returning to your store to shop more.

Remember, gifts don't have to be anything fancy. People just like getting free stuff—period. You can even throw in overstock inventory items that aren't selling well. Anything you add to the package will increase the perceived value of your transaction. It will leave your customer feeling positive and make her enthusiastic about returning to shop with you again.

eBay's Rules Concerning Advertising Gifts

If you're offering a gift as a deal-sweetener and not purely as a goodwill gesture after the transaction has closed, you should familiarize yourself with a few eBay regulations on the practice:

- For listings with multiple quantities, if you advertise a gift as a bonus to the item being sold, you must have an equal number of gifts to match the quantity for sale. Everyone who purchases the item must receive the same gift.
- If your bonus gift is given conditional on a certain bid amount, you must state that amount in the description. For example, if you give a free car stereo conversion kit for every MP3 player that sells for more than $200, you must state that amount. It doesn't suffice to say, "I'll throw in a car converter if the bidding goes high enough."
- If the gift does not add significant value to the item being sold, you can't mention it in the keyword title of the listing.

To learn more, visit eBay's help page concerning bonuses at http://pages.ebay.com/help/policies/listing-bonuses.html.

Other Promotions to Bring Customers Back

By now, your mind may be churning out different ways to promote your business and encourage buyers to return. Get creative with your promotions. Think of traditional brick-and-mortar retailers and the tactics they use. Here are a few ideas to get those creative juices flowing:

- *Think seasonal.* Let your customers know about holiday merchandise, back to school, Christmas in July, Latvian Independence Day, and other seasonally offered merchandise. Your options are endless.
- *Offer loyalty discounts.* Offer coupons for discounts or for free shipping on return business.
- *Use tell-a-friend promotions.* Your current customers are great resources for finding new customers. Offer them referral bonuses or other gifts in exchange for new business.

Include your promotions in your newsletter and/or e-mail them directly to your customers. Promotions encourage buying behavior. Sometimes all it takes is a gentle nudge to keep them interested and buying. Remember the elliptical customer life cycle—promotions bring customers back to roll through the cycle again.

Creating Return Incentive with MyStoreCredit.com

MyStoreCredit is a new third-party service that makes it simple to offer a financial incentive for your buyers to return to shop more. This ingenious service automatically establishes a store credit for your buyers based on the amount that they spend on their first purchase. This credit can be used toward future purchases from your eBay Store or listings. Sellers have the ability to set their own schedule of credit amounts based on a range of initial purchase prices.

Once the buyer opts-in for the MyStoreCredit system, she will periodically receive e-mailed updates from MyStoreCredit reminding her of her credit balance. It also includes links to 12 of your current listings (with the option of up to 60 links for an additional fee). When the buyer makes her subsequent purchase, her credit is refunded automatically via PayPal or manually through a check that you include with her shipment. All store credits are managed automatically through the service, so driving return traffic to your eBay business requires virtually no effort on the part of the seller. Visit http://www.mystorecredit.com for more information.

Other third-party services offer similar online promotional coupons. They allow sellers to create their own promotions and set specific codes that are redeemable through PayPal purchases:

- **Paycodes** http://www.paycodes.com
- **Aucsy** http://www.aucsy.com
- **Aucser** http://www.aucser.com

Recap

The key to customer retention and service is easy if you think of your business as a dialog with your customers and prospects. When you sustain a valuable conversation, you stay connected and available for whatever opportunity may materialize. Nobody knows where the next great business opportunity is going to come from. It could come from:

- A partner
- A friend
- A business acquaintance
- Someone who was just forwarded your newsletter
- An ancient customer
- Someone looking over the shoulder of the person reading your newsletter
- A prospect

There are so many different possibilities. Newsletters, gifts, and other promotions keep you in the game and in the minds of your audience.

Chapter 7

Take It to the Next Level: Charting Your Course, Measuring Success, Planning for the Future

---

"Where do I go from here?" may be a question you're asking yourself after reading the preceding chapters of this book. Hopefully, your mind is churning with great ideas to improve your eBay business and increase profits. If we've done a particularly good job, you may be so full of great ideas that you feel a bit puzzled as to where to start.

Well, have no fear, as this chapter will help you sort it all out. We'll show you how to

- Take the lessons from this book and create a plan of action.
- Set goals and timelines for implementing strategies.
- Measure your success.
- Improve what works.
- Plan for growth.
- Continue to learn and improve your business.

Charting Your Course

Imagine you're taking a trip to a place you've never been before. Wouldn't it be nice to have a map to help you get there? Or, even better, wouldn't it be great to have detailed directions that identify landmarks along the way so that you know you're headed in the right direction? Creating a successful marketing strategy for your eBay business is like planning a road trip. If you take the time to make a plan and chart your course, you're more likely to end up where you want to be. It's easy to do if you follow a few basic steps.

Pack Your Bags

Successful marketing strategy requires that you take a variety of approaches and mix them together into one cohesive plan. Think about how you pack for a trip. You want the right combination of underwear, outerwear, and footwear for your journey, but you don't want to include everything but the kitchen sink. You don't rely on one strategy; you need to use a few to get you to your destination with comfort, efficiency, and style. The combination of multiple economical efforts will yield optimum success.

Go back through the chapters of this book and scan the subheads. Make a list of every idea or strategy you feel could work for your eBay business. Remember that it's what you carry in your baggage as well as what you leave out that makes for a good marketing strategy. It's not enough to build your brand if you don't follow it up with customer retention efforts. You need strong item descriptions and the right inbound links to your listings, but you don't want to go overboard with meandering irrelevance and clutter.

Sit down, grab a pen and paper, and create a list of strategies and ideas as you go through the book. Think of it as your packing list for a profitable journey. Keep the following key concepts in mind as you review each chapter.

Chapter 1: Make a Plan

Don't take this chapter lightly. Remember the five basic considerations:

- Know who you are.
- Know your products.
- Know your customers.
- Know your competition.
- Know how to tie it all together.

If you didn't take notes or nail down these basic considerations the first time around, go back and spend time doing it now. This is the cornerstone to your success, and the remaining marketing efforts rely on this analysis.

Chapter 2: The eBay Seller's Toolbox

Consider tools you're already using and examine others that could make a difference in the way you do business. Can some tools save you time or effort? Which tools have the best potential to boost your sales?

Chapter 3: Putting a Face on Your eBay Brand

What steps can you take to create a cohesive brand image? How can you improve the design of your eBay listings and eBay Store? Can you improve your printed materials and packaging supplies?

Chapter 4: Sell Anyone Anything with Words

Consider the secrets of professional advertising copywriters and how you can implement them in your item descriptions. Recall the importance of creating headlines, using a conversational tone, listing FAQs, and selling persuasion. How can you jazz up your item titles to produce maximum search results?

Chapter 5: Advanced Marketing Strategies

You'll find plenty of sales-boosting gems in this chapter. How can you leverage your authority and expertise? How can you use scarcity to your best advantage? What about using testimonials or cross-selling your merchandise?

Chapter 6: Customer Satisfaction and Retention

Analyze your current customer service policies. What works? What needs improving? How can you generate repeat business? What promotions can you offer? What gifts can you give? How can you personalize your customer relationships?

Create Action-Oriented Lists

When you make your list, phrase your notes as action-oriented tasks. Don't just write something like "Improve my brand image." Rather, list the steps involved to accomplish this—here's an example:

1. Hire a designer to create a logo.
2. Print business cards and letterhead.
3. Use Listing Designer to spiff up my item listings.
4. Design my eBay Store with custom headers.

Focus on phrasing your list items to be performance-based, rather than outcome-based. If you *perform* the list of tasks, the natural *outcome* will be an improved brand image.

Create a Timeline for Success

After going through each chapter, you should have created a long list of ideas, tasks, and strategies. Perhaps it's so long that it boggles your mind. It's important that you not try to implement this list all at once. It will quickly become overwhelming, and you'll have no way of gauging which strategies have worked well and which haven't. You're better off creating a timeline to guide you in implementing different strategies. Recall our discussion about charting a course. Introducing individual tasks and efforts in a scheduled timeline is your map to success. The incremental efforts on a daily, weekly, and monthly basis are the landmarks.

Try this exercise:

1. Think about the marketing efforts that you can implement in the next week, over the next month, or within the next year.
2. Prioritize the items on your list. Highlight those that you suspect will result in the most profit or that you can execute with a high degree of success.
3. Identify areas of your business that need immediate improvement. Focus on tasks that help the process.
4. Separate items that require concerted effort and concentration versus simple tasks that can be implemented easily.
5. Take out your calendar or some paper and plan out a schedule for implementing your strategies.
6. Plan your timeline with monthly, weekly, and daily tasks. Choose the "bigger picture" strategies for the monthly efforts, and then break those down into weekly and daily tasks that will help you implement the strategies into your business.
7. Remember your luggage for the journey when creating your timeline; be sure to pack the right mix of tools and strategies from the different areas discussed in these chapters to optimize your success.

Set Goals

Goals consist of long-term vision combined with short-term motivation. The basic formula for setting a goal is this:

Timeframe + Performance = Outcome

An example of this formula for use in an eBay business is shown here:

In the next month (timeframe) + I will write stronger item descriptions (performance) = To increase my sales by 10 percent (outcome)

We all intellectually understand the value of setting goals, but few of us ever truly set them. Sure, we make New Year's resolutions that fade by February or we set unattainable or luck-based goals like "I'd like to win the lottery." Some of us just don't set goals at all out of fear of failure or due to laziness. Studies have shown that less than five percent of the population engages in formal goal-setting. Only one percent actually plans out goals, writes them down, and follows up to be sure they're executed. It should come as no surprise that the people who make up that goal-setting one percent are among the most successful and highest achieving members of society.

Every person reading this book has a similar goal in common: you want to make your eBay business more profitable. Heck, "Creative Strategies to Boost Profits Now!" is emblazoned on the cover of this book, and that may have enticed you to buy it. (We thank you, by the way!) However, just *reading* this book isn't going to boost your profits. You need to decide exactly what you want to achieve with your eBay business and make a step-by-step plan to get you there.

Earning more money with your eBay business may be the ultimate goal, but to achieve it, you need to create smaller goals that you can reach in increments. These subgoals should be challenging but definitely attainable, set in a specific timeframe, and they should have a series of tasks or even smaller goals that get you there.

Base these subgoals on the seven steps and chapters of this book, for example:

- Build a brand image.
- Write persuasive item descriptions.
- Improve your customer service.

Even the process of setting goals is a goal unto itself. You can also set goals based on the following:

- Setting specific amounts of increased profits or sales volume
- Finding ways to spend less time on eBay and more time with your family
- Being recognized as a leader in the eBay community
- Moving up to become a Gold-level PowerSeller

Every seller defines success differently. Take the time to figure out and write down your true goals, breaking them into smaller goals and performance tasks. Plug them into a timeline and you have a formula for success.

Finally, review your goals and activities on a daily basis. The key to achieving your goals is not just to set them, but also to perform continued goal review on a daily basis to make sure that you're staying on track. (Read this last part again, because it's important.)

Write It Down

Unwritten goals are nothing more than wishes. This statement isn't just fortune cookie fodder—it is gospel for successful goal-setting. *It is absolutely essential that you write out your goals and plan out your tasks and timeline on paper.* It helps create clarity about your goals and helps you visualize their achievement. Something about the act of writing creates a commitment; it's like making a contract with yourself. Your written goals and plan of action are your roadmap to success. Plan well, refer to your goals frequently, and enjoy the ride.

Analyze Your Return on Investment

Corporate "suits" have long touted the virtues of analyzing ROI, or *Return on Investment*. Essentially, you analyze the extent to which a purchase or specific project consumes resources and compare that to the additional revenue that's created.

This may sound simple, but it's not. Connecting revenue to inputs is difficult. And, ROI also factors in cost savings, labor savings, productivity enhancements, and efficiency gains that aren't always easy to quantify.

Don't sweat it too much, though. For our purposes, you don't need to get out your abacus or slide rule to calculate your ROI. We just want you to assess your decisions logically and track the various positive and negative outcomes you witness.

You don't need to get out your abacus or slide rule to calculate your ROI. We just want you to assess your decisions logically and track the various positive and negative outcomes you witness.

Understanding Your Investment

Every marketing strategy and effort you make to improve your eBay business will have two associated *costs*: time and money. This is your *investment*. Look over your list of goals and the tasks associated to reach those goals. Whether it is additional eBay fees incurred for extra services, expenses associated with promotions, or costs involved in printed branding materials, just about any marketing effort you make comes with a price tag.

Every effort you make also requires an investment of your time. Activities such as crafting persuasive item descriptions, writing a newsletter, or adding personalized touches to customer correspondence might not cost anything in dollars, but it does require that you spend extra time (or your employees' time, which you pay for, so it has an associated financial cost, too).

Understanding Your Return

Every marketing strategy and effort you make to improve your business will also have two associated *outcomes*: time and money. This is your *return*. Take, for example, eBay's Selling Manager Pro. This service costs $15.99 a month, but it has great potential to save you time managing listings, automating correspondence, and generating sales reports. And the time that you gain from this investment has a correlated monetary return, as you now have extra time to spend doing more profitable activities. Investments of time, such as writing great item descriptions, have the financial payoff of persuading buyers to bid higher or buy more, thus increasing your profit margins.

The key is to test and measure every strategy you implement. This is where it's helpful to have a timeline of tasks and activities. When you stagger your efforts into smaller steps, it's much easier to judge each step's effectiveness. Understand the investment of time and money involved in each effort and then compare those costs to the benefits they generate.

It should be noted, however, that ROI calculation is really just an estimate. It is difficult to make the results of these examinations totally quantifiable. Perhaps you'll see a 50 percent profit increase after implementing one strategy or another, but there may be external factors associated with the increase. The increase could also be prompted by seasonal sales peaks, a new demand for or scarcity of what you sell, and other factors outside of the individual strategy you've implemented. This is definitely more art than science. It's a bit like the story of The Three Bears—sometimes it will be too hot and sometimes too cold, and other times it will feel just right (that's when you know you've uncovered a winning strategy).

Large eBay sellers with the resources and bodies to throw at ROI analysis will be able to identify trends and returns more specifically. They can afford to test, test, and retest over long periods of time in much the same way advertisers and advertising agencies do. For example, companies with large transactional databases and business analysis software can slice and dice their sales data by time periods, product categories, seasonality, actual sales, and other factors. They're much more likely to connect a specific marketing activity to a specific bump (or decline) in sales. Small- to medium-sized eBay businesses with large amounts of data can identify these types of trends over time without using fancy software. Some sellers get a feel for what works and what doesn't, but they're really just responding to actual observations of testing over time. It's called *experience*.

A Few Tips on Time Management

Developing a new marketing strategy takes time. So you need to get a handle on how you spend it. Here are a few tips for effective time management:

- *Prioritize your activities.* Make a daily "To Do" list and highlight those tasks that are essential to complete.
- *Create routines.* Set specific times for certain tasks that recur daily, such as shipping, customer communication, and item listings and management.

- *Find ways to save time.* Find and use the services in your Seller's Toolbox that can help you cut corners without compromising quality.
- *Delegate tasks.* If you have employees, use them to their fullest. If you work alone, remember that while it's nice to run the show, you don't have to perform every act. Do-it-yourself works only when you enjoy doing the task at hand. Hire a designer if creating your own graphic identity isn't your cup of tea. Open a UPS account if you hate schlepping packages to the post office every day.
- *Beware of "time bandits"—personal phone calls, net surfing, chat rooms, computer games.* These distractions are fun, but they seriously eat into money-making time.
- *Schedule downtime into your day.* Give yourself a little time to enjoy a few of those time bandits as a guilty pleasure. If necessary, set an egg timer to help limit your downtime, and then get back to work!

Improving What Works

Performing ROI analysis on your marketing activities helps you identify winning business strategies and helps you weed out the losers. For those that don't succeed, take some time to "autopsy" the failure. Try to figure out exactly what went wrong. Ask yourself the following questions:

- Was the cost involved too high?
- Was the product not right for my particular niche market?
- Did it take too much of my time?
- Did my customers not respond as I expected?

Understanding why something didn't work will help you avoid similar errors in judgment in the future.

As to the winning strategies you uncover, make the same determinations as to why they succeeded. Incorporate these winning strategies into your daily eBay activities to ensure your continued success. Examine ways that these winning strategies can be expanded and improved. Go back to the section of this book where the strategy is discussed, and see whether other ideas could yield similar success. Figure out ways to take these strategies even further—or, as this chapter title suggests, to the next level.

Enforce Best Practices

If you have employees—1, 20, or 500—you'll need to seriously address the ways you communicate and enforce the gems of business wisdom you develop as you conquer the eBay universe. What you glean from ROI analysis needs to be translated into best practices that employees can easily follow. Even if you're a one-person shop, you'll need to write down what works and make sure you religiously review it and live by it.

For example, if you find out that your listings (for identical items, time-frames, and price ranges) receive five times more bids if you answer e-mail questions within one hour, then you need to enforce that as a best practice. Other best practices may relate to the following:

- Shipping speeds
- Inclusion of premiums
- Item description tones and attitudes
- Punctuality
- Customer follow-up
- Promotional offers

The list could go on and on. Customer follow-up is the area where you'll really see the biggest results. When you maintain consistent, proactive, superior customer-service levels across your organization, you build a dynamite business one customer at a time.

Plan for Growth

Picture it now: You have a successful marketing strategy in place, sales are booming, and you're racking up incredibly high profits. Perhaps you're already planning a luxurious tropical vacation or shopping for a new Jaguar XLS. Before your fantasies get out of check, you must remember the reality of many small businesses experiencing success and growth—namely, *surges in sales can really make you "stretch" your current capabilities and resources.* Keep in mind that some stretches are so intense that they can cause otherwise viable businesses to reach the breaking point.

Growth is wonderful, but it must be managed. You'll definitely encounter some growing pains when you try to vault to the next level with your business. To avoid the pitfalls, you want to invest some forethought and planning. This section covers some of the most common issues that arise when small businesses experience sudden growth and offers ways to handle such situations.

The first step in a growth policy is not to decide where and how to grow. It is to decide what to abandon.

—*Peter Drucker*
business management guru

Hiring Employees or Adding Team Members

One of the first side effects of a sales boom is the desperate feeling of being understaffed. If you work alone, this can feel especially overwhelming, as keeping up with a sales boom can be mentally and physically exhausting. If you have employees, you may notice that they're feeling a bit disgruntled at the sudden rise in your expectations of their performance and efficiency. (Profit-sharing can definitely ease this employee malaise, but remember that they're still only human, and it's unfair to expect superhuman performance to keep up with a sales boom.)

Note: If you want to read more about hiring, *Running a Successful Franchise*, by Kirk Shivell, (McGraw-Hill, 1993) has a good section on recruiting and supervising dependable employees.

Despite the overwhelming feeling of being understaffed, try not to rush your decision to hire employees or hire *more* employees. You want to be sure that your sales surge is sustainable so that you won't need to lay off workers in the future. Or, if you know that your sales boom is a short-term phenomenon (such as a holiday rush), hire employees who understand that their position is only temporary. All kinds of businesses are specifically geared for short-term outsourcing of tasks like accounting, billing, general organization, and other professional services. Many have flexible pay-as-you-go programs designed for small businesses.

Look for qualified temporary staff and even interns through the following sources:

- http://www.kellyservices.us
- http://www.manpower.com
- http://www.accountemps.com

You can also hire *virtual assistants* (sometimes called *virtual office temps*) that handle office support and other, more complex tasks via phone, e-mail, instant messenger, FAX, and even PCAnywhere, which is software that allows you to access computers remotely over the Internet. These workers can do everything from shipping and Web design to errand running and copy editing. Do a Web search to learn more about these kinds of employees, as this is a developing trend. Another good place for temp resources is Craigslist (http://www.craigslist.org), a great resource for those who live in or near metropolitan areas of the United States.

Freelance employees also list their services for hire on eBay's Professional Services page. Included are professionals in a variety of fields, including accounting, administrative, graphic and Web design, business strategy, software development, and much more. For information, visit http://pages .ebay.com/business_services. The page is created in conjunction with freelance specialists Elance. You can visit Elance's Web site (http://www.elance.com) directly to find freelance assistance, too.

Even though you may feel the urge to find any warm body to fill the gap, take the time to screen potential employees carefully. Think of the process as "team building." You want the best players you can find—and you need to be sure that they can work together. You and your employees will spend many hours together, so make sure that you have good personality matches along with strong work ethics and abilities.

Research all the costs involved in hiring employees. Don't forget that it's not just their wage you'll need to pay—there is the matter of payroll taxes, worker's compensation insurance, employee benefits, and other expenses. There is also a cost involved (both monetary and time) in training new employees and getting them up to speed. You may also need to invest in additional equipment, such as extra computers or upgrading your workspace to accommodate new employees. A good rule of thumb to follow is that an employee will cost your business at least *double* what you pay them in wages.

Finally, remember that as your business evolves, you must evolve, too. Your role will change from the doer to the leader. When many small business owners experience growth and add employees, they often have difficulty "letting go" of the smaller tasks that they used to do themselves. The shift from micro- to macro-managing can be tough, but it is essential to the viability of your business (and to your sanity, too).

The Joys of Going Solo

One of the most attractive aspects of running a small eBay business is that you can stay lean, mean, and *solo*. Going it alone has lots of advantages that are often overlooked.

Generally, people tend to deem businesses successful when they hire lots of employees and generate a lot of revenue. But it's really profitability that counts! Who cares about size when you can keep it small and stay flexible, agile, and margin-focused.

With a solo shop, you have all the advantages of speed to market and rapid adjustment, but you also don't have to worry about bad hiring decisions, payroll issues, burdensome accounting chores, theft, lawsuits, and insurance coverage. You also enjoy a lot of personal flexibility. If you want to leave the office to get a latté, you don't have to worry about employees slacking off while you're gone. You're the only one slacking off!

Keeping Up with Demand: Sourcing Inventory

Another problem with a sales boom is managing to keep enough inventory in stock to meet the demands of your customers. You need to make sure that your suppliers can keep up with your orders; and if they can't, you need to find new suppliers.

Remember that most wholesalers offer price breaks for retailers when they purchase large quantities of goods. Do your research and stay on top of different suppliers' prices as your sales volume and your wholesale orders increase. Leverage the increased volume of your wholesale orders to minimize the costs you pay per unit of goods.

You'll also need to find new and interesting goods to keep your return customers coming back to your eBay Store. What good are your customer retention efforts if you're not offering any new and enticing merchandise for return customers to purchase? The following are a few tips on sourcing inventory.

Note: What Do I Sell (http://www.WDISReports.com) is an eBay Certified Provider that specializes in teaching online auction sellers creative, professional strategies for sourcing inventory. They also offer techniques for selecting products to sell on eBay, locating legitimate suppliers, and effectively selling in the eBay marketplace.

Go to Trade Shows

Trade shows are wonderful places to find new merchandise, gather information on pricing, and establish relationships with wholesalers. They give you the opportunity to view merchandise in person. They spark creative ideas about new items you can add to your inventory line. Plus, they're just a heck of a lot of fun—they're truly a shopper's paradise, with the added bonus of sourcing inventory to improve your eBay business!

Merchandise trade shows occur throughout the country. Most involve a preregistration process, so you need to plan ahead to know when they're coming to a city near you. Here's a list of general merchandise trade show organizations and links to their Web sites:

- **ASD AMD Merchandise Shows**   http://www.merchandisegroup.com
- **Western Exhibitors**   http://www.weshows.com
- **Trans World Exhibits**   http://www.transworldexhibits.com

Trade shows of specialized merchandise also abound—from fashion, sporting goods, holiday items, food and gourmet goods, crafts—the list is virtually endless. If you sell in a specialized niche, research trade shows devoted specifically to your field of expertise.

Visit Gift and Merchandise Marts

Many cities have permanent gift and merchandise marts, in which wholesalers operate showrooms where retailers can view samples and order in volume. These marts also host a schedule of visiting tradeshows. A complete list of cities with specialty wholesale trade marts, along with links to each mart's Web site, is available at http://www1.buylink.com/marts/index.htm.

The added benefit of visiting trade shows or gift marts is that it puts you in touch with sales representatives from merchandise companies. It's their job to connect you with inventory. They will send you catalogs and come to you with offerings of new merchandise, making inventory sourcing an easy task for you.

Note: Some trade show reps and gift marts sell only to vendors with brick-and-mortar shops. Fortunately, such policies are becoming less common. If you find a product line that interests you but policy prevents access, don't let this deter you. Be persistent, and show them your sales volume and sell-through rates. Show them that you're willing to place large orders. When they recognize your potential, they may just change their tune.

Use the Internet to Source Inventory

Opportunities exist to source inventory on the Web, too. Web sites such as Buylink Marketplace (http://www.buylink.com) showcase thousands of merchandise wholesalers. You can search for items thematically or by individual vendor. You can even search by price range on products and download complete catalogs from specific vendors to source inventory from your desktop.

Also consider drop-shipping possibilities with Internet wholesalers. Two of eBay's Certified Service providers, Wholesale Marketer (http://www.wholesale-marketer.com) and Worldwide Brands (http://www.worldwidebrands.com/ebay), offer access to online wholesalers with thousands of products in a broad variety of niche markets. These goods can be purchased directly at bulk wholesale prices, or you can have the goods drop-shipped directly to your customers. Instead of purchasing the inventory, you simply list it for sale in your eBay Store, and when a customer purchases the goods, you place an order with the wholesaler and it ships the product directly to your customer. No storage, no warehouses, no cash on the barrel head—just profit in your pocket.

Buy Inventory Through eBay Wholesale Lots Categories

Product wholesalers have joined the eBay community and are selling their wares to other eBay sellers. Take advantage of this opportunity to find new inventory—all from the comfort of your office. Many categories offer "wholesale lots" as a subcategory. A complete list of wholesale lot categories is available at http://pages.ebay.com/catindex/catwholesale.html.

Automatically Scour eBay for Overlooked Bargains

Some sellers troll for scarce or rare goods on eBay, searching for items that were miscategorized or misspelled by less experienced sellers. While this can be time-consuming, the potential to turn a profit on what would otherwise be a high-bidding item can be great. There's a nifty little free tool called Fat Fingers (http://www.fatfingers.com) that helps you search for items with misspellings on eBay. Just type in the correctly spelled word and Fat Fingers generates a search on dozens of possible misspellings of the word.

This particular approach is useful when you're looking to find antiques and rare collectibles. Thousands of lay sellers pop up on eBay every day selling stuff from their garages. If you can find their misspelled valuables, you're one step ahead of the next buyer.

Explore Options to Sell for Others

Consigning items for sale is another option for finding great inventory. eBay's Trading Assistant program allows you to register as someone willing to sell goods for others in your area. For more information, visit http://www.ebay.com/ta.

The recent success of storefront businesses, like iSold It and Auction Drop, that consign goods for eBay sale led eBay to begin its Trading Post program. Trading Post is essentially a Trading Assistant who operates a staffed storefront with regular drop-in hours, where no appointment is necessary for consigning goods. To qualify as a Trading Post business, you must have a feedback score of 500 or higher, 98 percent positive feedback, and monthly sales of at least $25,000. As a Trading Post, your listings are prioritized to the top of the list in search results (and you get a special icon with your user ID). This adds visibility and credibility to your Trading Post business.

Allow Your Customers to Trade in Their Goods

Many traditional retailers have long known the power of customer trade-ins to source inventory and generate more sales. You frequently see this practice used in book and music stores, camera shops, sporting goods stores, and, of course, car dealerships.

There's a nifty new eBay tool that allows you to utilize this sourcing and sales tactic. The Trade-In System, created by eBay Certified Provider Infopia, is an automated system whereby potential buyers enter the specific details of the item they'd like to trade-in. From this information, a trade-in value is assigned to the preowned goods. Then the buyer shops for the new merchandise they desire and ships the preowned goods to the seller.

When the item is received, the value is credited toward the purchase of new goods. Not only is this a fantastic way to source inexpensive inventory, but it also encourages buying behavior. More information can be found at http://www.infopia.com/products/tradein.shtml.

Figure 7-1 shows the Web site for Dallas Golf, a Titanium PowerSeller that buys approximately a third of all used golf clubs in the country. The company has increased revenue by more than 200 percent using Infopia's Trade-In System.

Figure 7-1   Titanium PowerSeller Dallas Golf's online trade-in form

Guerilla Sourcing

A large portion of the eBay seller's community falls under the heading "guerilla sourcers." These sellers are like bloodhounds, with their noses to the ground, sniffing out goods to resell from such places as:

- Estate sales and garage sales
- Flea markets and swap meets
- Local auction houses
- Thrift and consignment shops
- Pawn brokers
- Dumpster diving
- Discount stores, outlets, and closeout franchises

Every seller who guerilla-sources inventory has her own secret hunting grounds for finding merchandise. However, no matter how full your sourcing bag of tricks may be, there's always room for improvement. If you get up at dawn to scour the flea market, consider arriving there an hour earlier and cruising the market with a flashlight in hand. Buddy up with the manager of your local closeout or discount store to see if he'll let you know the days when new inventory arrives. Develop a special relationship with that garbage collector who works the ritzy neighborhoods. Offer your expertise with charity thrift shops to help them identify valuable donations in exchange for consigning them for sale in your eBay Store. (If you offer them a percentage of the profit, they'll make more money for the charity and you'll get first crack at the goods.)

The possibilities are endless. When you get right down to it, it's really about hard work, cleverness, and a drive to beat the next guy to that diamond in the rough.

Analyze Your Resources and Equipment Needs

When your business grows, you usually need to expand your business's fixed assets. The physical constraints of your equipment and workspace become apparent after a sales boom. We mentioned this earlier in our discussion about the costs involved in hiring employees. But even if you continue to work alone or maintain your current staff level, you may need to invest in faster computers or better equipment. You may also need to move to a larger or more efficient workspace to keep up with the demands of your success. Equipment and location upgrades can be really expensive, so it's essential that you consider these factors when planning the growth of your eBay business.

Secure Capitol for Growth

We've all heard the old adage, "It takes money to make money." All the other factors of growth discussed in this chapter have a major component in common: they all take money. And you have to plan for how you're going to pay for it all.

A common pitfall that many businesses experience is an inability to manage their cash flow. When sales are up and the money is rushing in, the temptation is to start reinvesting wildly. While the instinct to reinvest is a good one, it can land you in financial trouble. In situations like this, many small businesses find that they're unable to pay the bills, even though they're enjoying huge profits.

Learn how to anticipate the peaks and valleys of sales throughout the course of a month. Remember that profit on paper is different than cash in hand. It's important to reinvest profits, but don't spend every penny you make. Know when and from where your cash needs come, and track your cash intake throughout the course of each month. Keep a cushion for unexpected expenses.

Consider securing outside financing to help manage your cash flow and grow your business. A secured loan or a line of credit can come in handy for investing in new equipment or inventory. Shop around for the best loan from local lenders, e-lenders, or the U.S. Small Business Administration. You can even secure financing through eBay. eBay's Seller Financing Program offers both secured loans and lines of credit. More information is available at http://pages.ebay.com/businesscredit.

Analyze Industry Trends

Without new markets and fresh products, there tends to be a ceiling to growth. In Chapter 1, we talked a little bit about identifying trends and turning them into opportunities. The subject deserves another mention here, because many businesses depend on their ability to identify and analyze trends.

Trend wavers, for example, follow hot items from niche to niche and market to market. They develop the experience and insight necessary to spot trends and stay ahead of what buyers are going to demand next month or even next year. Once they have a firm grasp of a particular market and its cycles, they can buy with more confidence and grow their particular position. The experience necessary to make big bets on fads and trends takes some time to develop; however, many sellers achieve great success on eBay with this kind of trend analysis strategy.

There are a number of different ways to gain trend analysis experience. The best and perhaps most expensive way to do it is through trial and error. You can supplement trial and error with some hedges, though. For example, you can analyze retail merchandising trends at popular department stores and figure out how to beat them at their own game. You can also frequent hip, off-the-beaten-track venues. Consider these locations known to be Meccas for hipsters:

- Melrose Avenue, Los Angeles
- Haight Street and Valencia Corridor, San Francisco
- Bleecker Street, Lower East Side, and SoHo, New York City
- King's Road and Knotting Hill, London
- Le Marais, Rue Bonaparte, Paris
- Shibuya-Ku, Tokyo

Just about any major city has its trendy spot(s). Keep an eye on what the young'uns are wearing, playing, and saying. Youth culture and street culture have their way of swimming into the mainstream.

If you're in the technology or electronics business, there are lots of great resources on the Web, via Podcast, (Internet broadcasts that are automatically downloaded to your iPod, portable MP3 player, or desktop media player), and even on the radio. Engadget (http://www.engadget.com) and Gizmodo (http://www.gizmodo.com) are on the leading edge of all things techie. Dozens of high-quality Podcasts analyze technology trends. (Check out the Gilmore Gang, the Engadget Podcast, and Slashdot Review. A quick Google search will lead you to these sites.) Leo Laporte, "The Tech Guy," hosts an AM radio show on weekends that covers technology trends, too.

You can follow stocks, too. Most companies now broadcast their quarterly earnings conference calls from their corporate Web sites. Just look up the company and follow the links to its earnings call audio files (for example, see Figure 7-2). Companies from cell phone makers to gown makers all discuss their trend analysis on the calls. Audio broadcasts of company conference calls are often archived on their Web sites. Usually they will keep the latest calls on the site for a month or so. After that, they're gone forever.

Don't forget to tap the usual resources, too. Your industry contacts can provide you with forward-looking hints. Trade newsletters often indicate the direction new markets are taking. The key is to develop your sources and do some back-scratching. Keep up with your communications, and make an effort to meet people who are on the inside. Think back to our niche discussions in Chapter 1. It's so important to know your niche and keep up with the competitive landscape. After all, when you stay ahead of the trends, you're essentially beating your competitors to the punch.

eBay is also a great resource for trend-spotting. eBay's "Hot Categories Report" gives you a monthly overview of the specific categories seeing the most bidding action. This list helps identify exactly where demand for items is currently exceeding the supply offered on eBay. Use the eBay "Hot Categories Report" to help guide your inventory purchasing decisions, and leverage

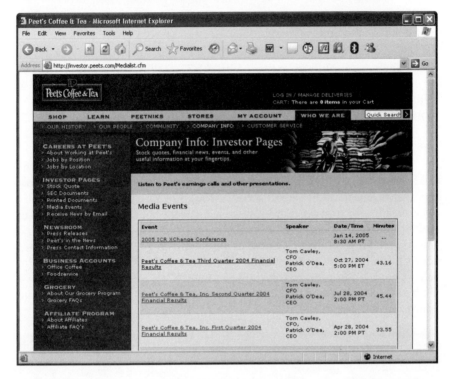

Figure 7-2   The link to the latest Peet's Coffee & Tea quarterly report is highlighted here.

the scarcity of your goods in your item descriptions. The eBay "Hot Categories Report" is available at http://pages.ebay.com/sellercentral/hotitems.pdf. (You'll need to have Adobe Acrobat installed to read the .pdf file.)

Continue to Learn

eBay is continually evolving, and to succeed, your business must continually evolve as well. Running a successful business, be it on eBay or in the world beyond, depends on your ability to keep your finger on the pulse of change and adapt quickly to meet new challenges. Fortunately, plenty of resources are out there to help.

Engage with the eBay Community

The eBay community can be an incredible resource for guiding you through the eBay system, no matter how experienced you are. A simple click on the Community button on the eBay toolbar links you to the eBay community at large. Use the resources available to stay on top of system changes and to continually gather information on how to improve your eBay business.

You'll also want to frequent external resources like those we mentioned in Chapter 2. eCommerce Guide (http://www.ecommerce-guide.com) and AuctionBytes (http://www.auctionbytes.com) are two sites that are particularly helpful. They keep you abreast of subtle changes on eBay and show you how to work smarter within the whole e-commerce context.

Discussion Boards, Chat Rooms, and the Answer Center

Visit discussion boards and the Answer Center to get help or assist others. It's truly amazing how helpful eBayers are. Information, ideas, and inspiration always seem to be shared generously. If you have a specific question or issue, create your own post, or browse the different boards to gain knowledge and insight from other sellers. Recent changes to the discussion boards allow you to search up to a year's worth of thread postings. This gives even more access to the wealth of information that eBayers share with each other. The Seller Central discussion board, shown in Figure 7-3, is one of the more active discussion boards on eBay. Dozens of other eBay topic and category topic boards are just like it.

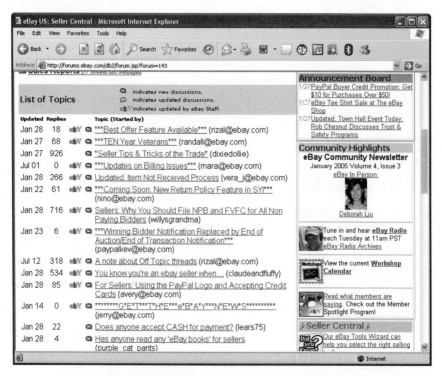

Figure 7-3   The Seller Central discussion board

News and Announcements

Take a quick peek at eBay's news and announcements boards each day, and scan the homepage each time you open eBay. This will help you stay on top of special offers that you can take advantage of and any system changes that you'll need to know about.

eBay Newsletters

eBay offers monthly newsletters that help you stay abreast of current activities and system changes to eBay. eBay's general community monthly newsletter, "The Chatter" (http://pages.ebay.com/community/chatter), is available online for any eBay user. There are also newsletters (both electronic and snail-mailed) available to PowerSellers. Read these newsletters religiously. They're full of useful and interesting tips and tidbits on improving your business.

eBay Workshops

eBay is continually offering free online workshops, hosted by special guests and expert eBay members on a variety of eBay subjects. The workshops take the format of a guest "lecture" combined with interactive comments from those participating in the workshop. Workshop discussions cover a wide range of subjects, from learning how to sell more efficiently, to using new tools, to category-specific discussions. Plus, you can read back through a year's worth of workshop archives.

eBay University

eBay University offers low-cost, fee-based courses, both online and in person, on improving your eBay business. For in-person instruction, a traveling team of eBay experts offers three different courses at cities around the United States. Online courses and CD-ROM courses are also available. More information is available at http://pages.ebay.com/university/.

eBay Live

eBay's annual convention, eBay Live, is an excellent opportunity for you to learn and network. The convention includes structured classroom activities and workshops to help you strategize your eBay success. It's also a trade show, hosting exhibitors with products and services that help you continually improve your eBay business. Finally, it's an opportunity to interact with other eBay sellers, to network and learn from each other. Traditionally held in June, eBay Live is hosted in a different city each year. More information is available at http://pages.ebay.com/ebaylive.

Use "Real-World" Resources

Many learning resources lie beyond the offerings of eBay and its community. Traditional venues such as the Small Business Administration (http://www .sba.gov), community colleges, and continuing education programs offer a plethora of information to help you guide and grow your business. If you aren't one already, become an avid reader. Don't just focus your learning with eBay-specific titles—expand your reading list to include general books on marketing and small business success.

Here's a list of suggested reading for improving your marketing and advertising techniques:

- *Ogilvy on Advertising,* by David Ogilvy
- *Tested Advertising Methods,* by John Caples
- *Guerilla Marketing,* by Jay Conrad Levinson

Here's a list of hot small business and marketing books:

- *Guerrilla Marketing in 30 Days,* by Jay Conrad Levinson and Al Lautenslager
- *What Customers Want: Using Outcome-Driven Innovation to Find High-Growth Opportunities, Create Breakthrough Products, and Connect with Your Customers,* by Anthony Ulwick
- *Before the Brand: Creating the Unique DNA of an Enduring Brand Identity,* by Alycia Perry and David Wisnom III
- *The One-Day Marketing Plan: Organizing and Completing a Plan that Works,* by Roman G. Hiebing and Scott W. Cooper

Recap

So we're at the end of the road here. You've read the most essential steps to building a thriving, profitable eBay business. You've been introduced to some of the most valuable tools known to the eBay universe. You learned what's critical in terms of visual technique. Some of the most enduring marketing strategies have been placed at your disposal. You got a long short-course in customer satisfaction. And you now have a concise reference for eBay marketing activities that will keep on supporting you as long as you keep on selling.

Not only do you have concise steps for improving your business, but you have this solid platform from which to take that leap. You can move up the ranks in PowerSeller status, command category hegemony, or even develop into a powerhouse corporate eBay distribution machine. These steps, tools, and resources give you the impetus, conviction, and concrete knowledge necessary for sustained eBay success.

What's more, you can build on this base and add to your experience. Mark up the pages and add your own thoughts. Keep your brainstorming scrap paper in between the pages as bookmarks. Take the concepts within these pages and run with them another 100 yards.

Your own creative energy and business acumen will take you farther down the road, and we'll definitely want to hear from you when you discover new strategies and tips. Join our eBay Group (eBay Marketing Success Strategies) to share your suggestions, tips, and tricks, and we'll make sure your contributions are noted and shared widely in the next edition. You'll find us by clicking the "Groups" link from the eBay Community page and searching on the name eBay Marketing Success Strategies. You can also enter the URL http://groups.ebay.com/forum.jspa?forumID=100024004. Be sure to check our Web sites for significant links and resources (http://www.JanelleElmsBooks .com, http://www.redfishantiques.com/ebaymarketing.html, and http://www .qualitywriter.com/ebaymarketing).

Finally, think about this before we part ways. All the big nonfiction business books say something similar—namely, successful business responds to change. Now that's kind of a boring, jaded quip, but it's true. Change is where it's at, especially in this hyper-drive Internet world. But change is superficial. Sure the ads are laid out in HTML rather than linotype. That's a big change. The visuals are JPEGs rather than plate photography. But the constants are timeless.

Persuasion is the oldest art (perhaps second only to pure athleticism and hunting prowess). Customers rule; discover their true needs and provide them solutions. Presentation has to fit the context and the need. Networking requires real human contact. You can't just put up a bunch of links and expect to be a hub of activity. Real success requires reasoned, logical planning. You can't meditate yourself to profits; you need to set goals and work toward them by checking off tangible tasks. And true joy is in the hunt, not the killing. Remember that, and you'll have the time of your life selling everything from bubble gum to iPods on eBay. It's so much fun to test, tweak, and discover on this wonderful digital bazaar. The stories you live and the people you meet will be reward enough; yet, the cash will be yummy, too.

So go forth and make your millions. Remember that 80 percent of eBay listings read like junk and look even worse. The bar is low, and with just a few targeted efforts, you can blow away your closest competitors. The top 10 percent eBay sellers make more than 90 percent of the money that flows through eBay! If you can improve your marketing skills and crank up your eBay business, you'll be on your way to greatness.

Happy selling!

Index

eBay Your Way to Success

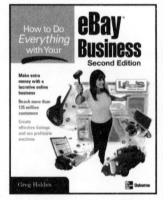